Why You Are a Liberal
—Or Should Be

Why You Are a Liberal
—Or Should Be

Keevan D. Morgan

iUniverse, Inc.

New York Lincoln Shanghai

Why You Are a Liberal—Or Should Be

iUniverse, Inc.

For information address:
iUniverse, Inc.
2021 Pine Lake Road, Suite 100
Lincoln, NE 68512
www.iuniverse.com

Edited by: Rosanne M. Ullman
Rosanne M. Ullman Better Writing Group

ISBN: 0-595-31354-X (pbk)
ISBN: 0-595-66300-1 (cloth)

Printed in the United States of America

This book is dedicated to my wife, Rosanne, and my daughters, Rebecca, Jaina, and Alanna, who prove that Liberals come in at least four different, wonderful personalities.

Contents

INTRODUCTION

It was my fascination with the American Civil War—something you catch young like a love of dinosaurs or puzzles—that led me to an unshakable embrace of Liberalism, *American* style. At some point, instead of viewing the Civil War as pageantry or gallantry, I really studied it. I came to understand, as one who grew up in Illinois—"the Land Of Lincoln," it says on our license plates—that this tectonic convulsion can be understood only as a victory for Liberalism, whose essence is the "proposition that all men are created equal," as Lincoln put it in the Gettysburg Address. This proposition was advanced and stood triumphant at the end of the Civil War through the power of our central, federal, government. In the same speech, Lincoln charged all Americans in future generations with the duty to carry on the fight for the proposition:

> It is for us the living, rather, to be dedicated here to the unfinished work which they who fought here have thus far so nobly advanced. It is rather for us to be here dedicated to the great task remaining before us—that from these honored dead we take increased devotion to that cause for which they gave the last full measure of devotion—that we here highly resolve that these dead shall not have died in vain—that this nation, under G-d, shall have a new birth of freedom—and that government of the people, by the people, for the people, shall not perish from this earth.

For the past 35 years or so, Liberals have had a great deal of trouble carrying out this unfinished work. Ironically, the challenge began on the heels of some of our great victories in the 1960s. Our limited progress resulted not from failed ideas, as Conservatives ardently argue, but because Conservatives talked longer, talked louder, and worked very hard to define the debate using the Conservatives' phony premise that "big government in Washington" is "the People's" *enemy*. To ascend again, we Liberals must now regroup and demonstrate the obvious, which is that in American history, the Federal government always has been, and remains, "the People's" *instrument* for protecting Lincoln's proposition.

American Liberalism has been on the defensive because we do not remember how we came into being or the purposes of our existence. We Liberals must reinvigorate ourselves, so that we can redefine the national debate on its true premise and, thereby, win it. This will allow the American people once again to utilize our national government for its proper purposes at home and abroad. Non-Liberals of goodwill must understand how they have been hoodwinked. Contrary to what they've been told, what passes as the Conservative "philosophy" has neither a respectable past nor the ability to keep this country great.

The primary American problem that Liberals have been addressing since the adoption of the Constitution is biblical in proportion and sense—simply, how to ensure that we both stop doing unto others what is hateful to ourselves, and start treating our neighbors as ourselves. Conservatives, who smugly swing their Bibles in scorn of their enemies, have failed at each and every step of the way for well more than 200 years to promote the Golden Rule. Instead, they have supported and profited from racism ever since Jamestown. They have stood in the way of virtually every attempt to use government for its proper Constitutional purpose of promoting the general welfare, although they are happy to have it promote their own. All that we Americans take for granted—Social Security, Medicare, anti-trust laws, securities laws, workplace safety laws, bank safety, child-labor laws, and food supply safety laws—have been opposed by Conservatives who label them a plot against "States' Rights and local control," or against individual freedom, or outright Bolshevism. Conservatives have never been *for* anything, except slavery, Jim Crow, trusts and other big-business ways of making rich men richer. Conservatives' entire culture is "anti." And, don't buy their newfound love of the military either. For almost all of our history, they were isolationists who ignored America's enemies.

Remember, Lincoln was talking about preserving a *government*. The "of, by, and for" was merely the type of government he wanted, and wanted us, to preserve. The Northern soldiers understood this. A month before dying at Gettysburg, one of them wrote that he was ready to die for the Northern cause:

for the purpose of crushing this d[amne]d rebellion and to support the best *government* on G-d's footstool.[1]

Because the Conservatives are against government, they have abjectly failed ever to promote a single constructive use *for* government. Therefore, it is up to us Liberals to deal with America's problems, because Conservatives won't, and never have, and never will.

We first have to overcome Liberalism's tendency toward soft thinking. Our creativity and bravery in dealing with the nation's problems sometimes lead to dead ends that we need to identify and exit faster in the future.

For example, Liberals may have continued to regulate a few industries no longer in need of it, and we've tolerated crooked union officials. This is nothing compared with the shameful history of Conservatives, who left behind the dead and maimed of slavery; the dead and maimed of the Civil War; the dead and maimed of the Reconstruction era; the lynched and maimed of the Jim Crow era; the dead and beaten of the anti-union era; the dead and tortured of the modern Civil Rights era; the hungry and cold children of pre-welfare times; the dead-ended women and minorities of the college quota-era; and the drugged and uneducated underclass we have warehoused in sardine can prisons. Don't get Liberals wrong—once the crime is committed, so is society committed to the offender's punishment. No Conservative will ever spend 10 minutes trying to figure out how to keep the inmates from ending up in prison in the first place, other than mouthing some platitude about going to church and listening to our parents. Those are fine things, and we Liberals are all for them, but the issue is about using Lincoln's *government* here, not developing a philosophy for personal success. Because Conservatives will never use the government, their election to office is a contradiction in terms; they are simply of no use to the problems confronting America, and they never have been.

When Conservatives finally accept Lincoln's proposition and use the federal government to protect the individual against other individuals and the states, when we have built a society of all "us" and not "them and us," only then can we do what the "intellectual" leaders of the Conservative movement would like—sit back and read the writings of classic English conservative Edmund Burke over tea and crumpets in order to determine the proper roles for our elected representatives in a republican form of government. At that

---

1. James M. McPherson, *What They Fought For* (Doubleday Dell Publishing Group, Louisiana State University Press, 1994), 33-4.

point we will be accomplishing our common goals for, through, and by the government.

So far, however, Conservatism has always been used for the opposite of its stated purpose of *limiting* government. From the beginning here in America, Conservatives' real purpose has been only to limit *one* government—the federal government—so that they can concentrate as much power as possible in the fewest possible number of white, well-to-do men as they can get away with at any particular time, holding sway from their state and local centers of despotism. Each advance from this race-based patriarchalism was opposed by Conservatives, and unless we Liberals get back in the driver's seat, we can all expect our Ship of State to be thrown into reverse. So history shows.

Reason 1. Liberals Support the Civil War-Inspired Modifications to the Constitution's "Original Intent."

It has been 138 years since the North won the Civil War, and yet our current debate largely stems from the issue that ignited the Civil War—race. That is why, newer states that were not yet formed aside, the "red" and "blue" states of the 2000 Presidential election are more or less divided along the "blue" and "gray" lines of the Civil War. How ironic it is that Lincoln's Republican Party, the party of strong federal intervention to correct state and local abuses of power, has been taken over by the ideological descendants of the traitorous Confederate President, Jefferson Davis. But Conservatives always have, and still do, reject Lincoln's Proposition, and therefore racism has necessarily followed as one of Conservatism's foundations.

Conservatism has gained ground during the past 35 years by falsely defining the debate as one over which side is best carrying out the Constitutional desires of "the Founding Fathers." Effective Liberalism was doomed the moment it agreed to this debate, because the essence of American Liberalism is the *rejection* of *some* of the Founding Fathers' basic premises. Liberals are the heirs of Abraham Lincoln, who, and whose armies, victoriously opposed the "States' Rights" system established by the Founding Fathers, substituting in its place a highly modified system of government in which the states, which had greatly abused their power, found that power rightfully and greatly diminished. This new system had and has a decidedly different purpose and methods from the defective one established by the Founding Fathers.

Conservatives will here be tempted to use this against Liberals. "See," they will say, "Liberals reject the American Revolution, and reject the United States Constitution." *No we do not.* The American Revolution and the United States Constitution are, respectively, a great event and a great document in the evolution of human freedom. However, each served as a way station in that evolution; neither was the destination. The American Revolution cannot be understood without recognizing that the defective Articles of Confederation had to be replaced by the Constitution, and the defective original Constitution cannot be understood without recognizing that we fought the Civil War—the bloodiest war in American history, losing 620,000 dead—to amend that document and to correct the ill-fated and ill-founded notion that states and local governments know best. Lincoln's victory substituted the fundamental premise that from that point forward, the *federal* government would be the protector of last resort of the individual's liberties and general welfare.[1] Article I, Section 2(3) of the original Constitution provided, in so many words, that African-Americans counted only 60% as much as white people when apportioning votes for the House of Representatives. Thus, the Conservatives' insistence upon "strict construction" of the Constitution is an outright fraud; that original Constitution was replaced by the post-Civil War Constitutional Amendments, which dedicated this country to the Proposition and changed the original Constitution accordingly.

Shamefully, Conservatives have, bit by bit, chipped away at Lincoln's great victory—the People's great victory—under the charge that Liberals believe in "Big Government." This accusation further distorts the actual disagreement between Liberals and Conservatives, because the debate is not over "small versus big" government, but over *which* government primarily should assist the People. Conservatives say that local governments and states should have more power, because they are closer to the people. Liberals posit that it is the federal government to which we should look, based both upon the historical *failures* of local and state government as opposed to the historical *achievements* of the federal government, and upon Lincoln's victory and the subsequent Constitutional Amendments wrought by that bloody triumph.

---

1. American casualties during the Civil War were: Federal—360,000; Confederate—260,000. *See* James M. McPherson, *What They Fought For* (Doubleday Dell Publishing Group, Louisiana State University Press, 1994), 27.

Let's take a stroll down memory lane and identify the ideas with which Conservatives have always aligned and continue to align. Conservatives dress up their thinking under the disguise of the "philosophy" of "limited government." More accurately, what this "philosophy" really means is "permission for local and state governments to govern oppressively."

Start with Thomas Jefferson, a Virginian, who planted the intellectual seeds of secession by selling his grandchildren the idea that "the government that governs least, governs best."[2] (Actually, he gave only some of his grandchildren this basis. He gave his African-American grandchildren the non-intellectual choice to remain in chains.) This sounds good in theory, because none of us wants troops quartered in our homes or searches conducted without probable cause and a warrant issued by a judge. The reality of this theory, however, was that Thomas Jefferson was able to continue to own other human beings, as could George Washington and the whole States' Rights crowd.

From 1789 until 1861, this country was torn by what was, and often still is, referred to as "Sectionalism." Let's get it right. Sectionalism was just another name for one side of the slavery debate. It was best said by firebrand Senator John C. Calhoun of South Carolina in an 1850 Senate speech: "I have Senators, believed from the first that the agitation on the subject of slavery would, if not prevented by some timely and effective measure, end in disunion."[3] Calhoun continued that "the first and great cause" of disunion was the exclusion of slavery in most of the territory added to the United States after independence.[4]

A decade after Calhoun's speech, Senator Louis Trezevant Wigfall opined that "you insist upon negro equality…and I say to you that we cannot live in peace, either in the Union or out of it, until you have abolished your abolition societies."[5] Or, as Senator Toombs from Georgia, whose post-Civil War Ku

---

2. The saying is widely ascribed to Jefferson, but its origin is not really known, according to http://faculty.virginia.edu/setear/courses/ilaw/leastdig.htm
3. Congressional Globe 31 Cong. 1 sess. (John Rives, Washington, D.C., 1850) 451-455 *passim*, March 4, 1950, as quoted in *American History Told By Contemporaries*, ed. Albert Bushnell Hart, 14th ed. (New York: Macmillan, 1968), 48.
4. *Ibid.*, 49.
5. *Ibid.*, 175.

Klux Klan paraphernalia I have seen in his nice home in Washington, Georgia, said in no uncertain terms:

> The Senator from Kentucky came to your aid, and says he can find no
> Constitutional right of secession. Perhaps not; but the Constitution is not
> the place to look for States' Rights. If that right belongs to independent
> States, and they did not cede it to the Federal Government, it is reserved to
> the States, or to the people. Ask you new commentator where he gets your
> right to judge for us. Is it in the bond?...In a compact where there is no
> common arbiter, when the parties finally decide for themselves, the sword
> alone at last becomes the real, if not the Constitutional arbiter.[6]

Alexander Stephens, the Confederacy's Vice-President, in a sort of historical anticipation of the Gettysburg Address that was still a few years down the pike, explicitly acknowledged that slavery was the immediate cause of the Civil War. He rejected the notion that all men are created equal, stating that the Confederacy:

> [i]s founded upon exactly the opposite idea; its foundations are laid, its cor-
> nerstone rests, upon the great truth that the negro is not equal to the white
> man; that slavery, subordination to the superior race, is his natural and nor-
> mal condition. This, our new government, is the first, in the history of the
> world based on this great physical, philosophical, and moral truth.[7]

It may have been the first, but as Nazi Germany attests, it wasn't the last. Yet Conservatives continue to defend the Confederate flag as a mere symbol of "heritage." Well, 320,000 died for the Liberal cause to abolish that flag and the evil institution and attitudes it supported. Heritage or no heritage, it is time to finish the job.

As another Union soldier wrote to his missionary parents after two wounds and a bout with typhoid [emphasis in original]:

> I say, better to let us all *die* fighting for *union* and *liberty*, than to yield one
> inch to these 'rebel slave mongers' as Charles Sumner justly calls them.[8]

---

6. *Ibid.*, 172
7. McPherson, 47-48.
8. *Ibid.*, 46

Or, as one of that soldier's compatriots put it:

> It tells me that while I am absent from home, fighting the battles of our country, trying to restore law and order, to our once peaceful & prosperous nation, and endeavoring to secure for each and every American citizen of every race, the rights guaranteed to us in the Declaration of Independence...I have children growing up that will be worthy of the rights that I trust will be left for them.[9]

As Senator Toombs noted, the "final arbiter" of the question was civil war, and at the conclusion of that the arbitrator entered a final non-appealable decision—the venomous doctrine of "States' Rights" was declared null and void. Conservatives have never accepted this defeat, and we Liberals have been forced to revive our victory in each generation.

Americans, like all people, try to put the best face on their own history; we do have to cut each other considerable slack for our different upbringings and backgrounds. But, this isn't true for slavery. Historians who merely label this period as one of "Sectionalism" and praise the great "compromises" of the period that kept the peace and the country together gloss over the one essential difference between the "Sections." One side harped on States' Rights and "local control," while the other side called for the "Peculiar Institution" of slavery to be destroyed by Washington—and I don't mean George. States' Rights and local control were excuses for our first 72 years as a means to keep in place a barbarous and uncivilized system of oppression. Localism meant the right to do evil to other people, pure and simple.

When Lincoln was elected, those "freedom" loving people rallying under the banner of States' Rights decided that the rights of their states were superior to actual human freedom and, therefore, it was time to force a war over the issue. Force it they did, choosing Jefferson Davis as their leader. Today's Conservatives want the President to have the "line item veto." It is no coincidence that Davis had it.

Davis shared another characteristic of many modern Conservatives: he equated personal integrity with public virtue. Davis should be given full credit for being a man of high personal integrity, with steadfast obedience to his conceptions of duty and a willingness to sacrifice everything for his beliefs, which included an overriding belief in an individual's freedom—well, those of

---

9.   *Ibid.*, 46

the white male, anyway. But, it is precisely these personal virtues, and his core belief in freedom, that make Davis and all of his followers, both past and modern, so completely and equally myopic. Davis was arrested near the war's end and chained in a dank cell by a cruel Union officer. Davis stoically accepted his fate, the chains were soon removed, and he was eventually freed.[10] Yet, the man never saw the connection between his chains and the chains, beatings, hangings, and rapes of African-Americans, or the connection between his dank cell and the dank slave floors upon which his human chattel shivered—products, along with millions of their forebears, of his "philosophy" of "limited government" and "States' Rights." Moreover, Davis lost all four of his sons to war or disease, again never making the connection between their deaths and the shivering illnesses and deaths of his own former slaves.

Davis's armies shared the same dichotomy of conduct as did he. The war was largely fought with soldiers respecting the rights of the other side's combatants and civilians; if anything, the Union Troops treated the Southern civilians worse than their Southern counterparts did Northern civilians, but then again the Southern soldiers did not have as many opportunities for such mistreatment. On the other hand, in the Gettysburg campaign, the Southern armies rounded up free African-Americans in the North and sent them into bondage in the South.[11] And, when the time came that the North finally put African-Americans into battle, Southern troops sometimes slaughtered them when captured. One such example was the "Fort Pillow" massacre. There is still some controversy as to exactly what the Confederate soldiers did there, but of the Union soldiers remaining after the battle, only 20% of the African-American troops were taken prisoner as against 60% of the white ones.[12]

The apologists of yesterday and today, including some African-Americans pushing their own form of "Sectionalism," try to gloss over the fundamental battle over the historical contexts and consequences of the States' Rights argu-

---

10. Shelby Foote, *The Civil War A Narrative, Red River to Appomattox* (New York: Vintage Books, A Division of Random House, 1974), 1033-1039.

11. Margaret Creighton, "Living on the Fault Line: African American Civilians and the Gettysburg Campaign," in *The War Was You and Me: Civilians in the American Civil War*, ed. Joan E. Cashin (Princeton: Princeton University Press, 2002), as reviewed by Lyde Cullen Sizer, "The War Is Messier Than That," for *H-CivWar*, June 2003, at http://www.h-net.org/reviews/showrev.cgi?path=113601059720050

12. Foote, 111-112.

ment. Instead, they present it as a battle over "preserving the Union," as if the battle were merely one to maintain the "territorial integrity" of the United States. Perhaps that was the broadest principle upon which all could agree in prosecuting the war, and it was more true at the beginning of the war. Not so coincidentally, the Union fought poorly at those stages of the war, because the South, the ignoble purposes of its "philosophy" aside, at least had one.

Lincoln well understood the irreconcilable dichotomy in the Southern position. Said Lincoln, "The *perfect* liberty they sigh for is the liberty of making slaves of other people."[13] The Southerners knew the real stakes, too—as demonstrated by the Southern soldier who wrote his fiancée that he was fighting to attain "a free white man's government instead of living under a black republican government."[14]

It was only when Lincoln, exercising theretofore unthinkable federal powers, proclaimed all the slaves free in areas in rebellion after the North "won" the indecisive battle of Antietam (the bloodiest day in Amercian history), that the Union, now armed with a moral imperative—the *Liberal* imperative to free the slaves—moved into high gear and vanquished the proponents of States' Rights, who were *the enemy* of the new nation Lincoln and his armies were building. Sure, Lincoln did not start out as "the Great Emancipator." He is well-known to have made many racist slurs in his life, and even had some crackpot ideas like sailing African-Americans back to Africa. But Lincoln overcame early errors to use the power of the United States federal government to overcome what was then the most pressing defect in the American system of freedom.

Therefore, when the Civil War ended, *so did the Constitution's "original intent."* Congress passed a series of Constitutional Amendments, including, of course, the abolition of slavery in the 13th Amendment. However, the 13th Amendment was just the frosting on the cake for our purposes, because slavery had already been effectively abolished. It is with the 14th Amendment that Liberalism has its birth certificate. The amendment says:

> All persons born in the United States, and subject to the jurisdiction thereof, are citizens of the United States and of the States wherein they reside. No State shall make or enforce any law which shall abridge the privileges and immunities of citizens of the United States, nor shall any State

---

13. *Ibid.,* 50 [emphasis in original].
14. McPherson, 53.

deprive any person of life, liberty, or property without due process of law;
nor deny to any person within its jurisdiction the equal protection of the
laws.

This was the definitive conclusion to the debate. States' Rights and "local
control" were placed on the ash heap of United States history. In their place,
the memories of hundreds of thousands of Union casualties and millions of
Union veterans supported the new system of federal government dominance
over the States and local units of government, which had shown they just
could not be trusted with protecting the freedom and general welfare of their
citizens and residents. Author and Civil War historian Herman Belz observes:

> In its national aspect American citizenship was a title to fundamental civil
> rights under the Constitution, such as the right to own property, which the
> Civil Rights Act identified. From this national right flowed the right as a
> state citizen to enjoy equality in respect of a state's criminal and civil code.
> Thinking in these terms, the Philadelphia *North American* refuted the idea
> that state and federal citizenship were separate legal entities; on the con-
> trary, they were essentially the same. [Philadelphia *North American*, April
> 11, 1866] According to Republican arguments in 1866, the federal govern-
> ment through the Thirteenth Amendment assumed power and responsibil-
> ity for protecting the civil rights surrounding personal liberty. The power
> was not primary, original, or direct, however, as in a unitary government,
> but rather corrective, supervisory, and indirect. It was intended to guaran-
> tee state performance in providing equality before the law with respect to
> ordinary civil rights. When states denied citizens' rights by enactments
> such as the Black Codes, or when they denied equal protection by failing to
> uphold rights or administer justice impartially, as occurred so egregiously in
> the 1870s, the federal government could intervene to secure civil rights. In
> substance and practical effect therefore, national citizenship consisted in
> equality before the law as a state citizen.[15]

Though triumphant, the Liberals were by far not thoroughly victorious. At
first, there was progress. An African-American took over Jefferson Davis's old
U.S. Senate seat.[16] There were attempts to spread the franchise among African-Americans in general and, regrettably, some attempts to keep it from

---

15.   Herman Belz, *Emancipation and Equal Rights, Politics and Constitution-
      alism in the Civil War Era* (W.W. Norton & Company, 1978), 120
16.   Foote, 1004.

former Confederates. With reform hanging in the balance, the North chose to sell out Liberalism in the 1876 Presidential election when, in order to garner the electoral votes for popular vote loser Rutherford B. Hayes, the Republicans agreed to withdraw federal troops from the South.

This gave States' Rights a new day. A former Confederate General, and a great one, Nathan Bedford Forrest, was the first Grand Wizard of the Ku Klux Klan.[17] In October 1871, General Grant was forced to suspend the writ of *habeas corpus* to deal with the KKK in nine counties of South Carolina. The Circuit Court of Columbia, South Carolina, then returned 785 true bills against Klan members, stating:

> *To the Judges of the United States Circuit Court:* In closing the labors of the present term, the grand jury beg leave to submit the following presentation: During most of the whole session we have been engaged in investigations of the most grave and extraordinary character—investigations of the crimes committed by the organization known as the Ku-Klux Klan. The evidence elicited has been voluminous, gathered from the victims themselves and their families, as well as those who belong to the Klan and participated in its crimes. The jury has been shocked beyond measure at the developments which have been committed, producing a state of terror and a sense of utter insecurity among a large portion of the people, especially the colored population. The evidence produced before us has established the following facts:...
>
> 4. That the Klan, in carrying out the purposes for which it was organized and armed, inflicted summary vengeance on the colored citizens of these counties, by breaking into their houses at the dead of night, dragging them from their beds, torturing them in the most inhuman manner, and in many instances murdering them; and this, mainly on account of their political affiliations. Occasionally additional reasons operated, but in no instance was the political feature wanting...[18]

And that was when African-Americans were *Republicans.*

---

17. "Ku Klux Klan," *The Columbia Encyclopedia*, 6th ed., 2001, *Bartleby.com*, at http://www.bartleby.com/65/ku/KuKluxKl.html
18. *Our Nation's Archive, The History of the United States in Documents*, ed. Erik A. Bruun and Jay Crosby (New York: Black Dog & Leventhal Publishers, 1999).

The Klan became so oppressive in Kentucky that a delegation of African-American citizens from Frankfort presented a formal complaint to Congress. Among the many listed horrors that those citizens had to endure were:

> 1. A mob visited Harrodsburg in Mercer County to take from jail a man named Robertson, Nov. 14, 1867; 2. Smith attacked and whipped by regulation in Zelun County Nov. 1867; 3. Colored school house burned by incendiaries in Breckenridge Dec. 24, 1867;…6. Wm. Pierce hung by a mob in Christian July 12, 1868;…10. Silas Woodford age 60 badly beaten by disguised mob. Mary Smith Curtis and Margaret Mosby also badly beaten, near Keene Jessemine County Aug. 1868;…13. James Parker killed by Ku Klux Pulaski, Aug. 1868;…17. F.H. Montford hung by a mob near Cogers landing in Jessamine County Aug. 18, 1868;…19. Negro hung by a mob Sep. 1868;…28. Two negroes shot by Ku Klux at Sulphur Springs in Union County Dec. 1868;…33. Spears taken from his room at Harrodsburg by disguised men Jan. 19, 1869;…37. Geo Bratcher hung by mob on sugar creek in Garrard County March 30, 1869;…40. Miller whipped by Ku Klux in Madison County July 2d, 1869; 41. Chas. Henderson shot and his wife killed by mob on silver creek Madison County, July, 1869;…49. Ku Klux whipped a negro at John Carmins's farm in Fayette County Sept. 1869;…52. Ku Klux ordered Wallace Sinkhorn to leave his home near Parkville Boyle County Oct. 1869;…56. Searcy hung by mob madison County at Richmond Nov. 4th, 1869; 61. Mob take two Negroes from jail Richmond Madison County one hung one whipped Dec. 12, 1869;…62. Two Negroes killed by mob while in civil custody near Mayfield Graves County Dec. 1869;…64. Negroes whipped while on Scott's farm in Franklin County Dec. 1869.[19]

The petitioning good citizens of Frankfort had noted in the body of their petition, "The Legislature has adjourned; they refused to enact any laws to suppress Ku Klux disorder."[20] This is just another instance why, in United States history, it is the central, federal, government to whom freedom lovers must turn, *not* the States, which pander to their lowest common denominator.

One after another, former Confederate States passed "Jim Crow" laws that established Southern-American apartheid. Included were "separate but equal" schools that were definitely the former, but hardly the latter. Among the many types of segregation laws were:

---

19. *Ibid.*, 408.
20. *Ibid.*, 407

Alabama—

☞ Barred white women from acting as nurses for black men.

☞ Mandated that whites and blacks have separate waiting and ticket purchasing areas in bus stations.

☞ Mandated that whites and blacks travel in separate railway cars or sections of railway cars.

☞ Mandated that whites and blacks eat in separate restaurants or segments of restaurants and if in the same restaurant, separated by a partition at least 7 feet tall.

☞ Banned blacks and whites from playing pool together.

☞ Mandated that blacks and whites have separate toilet facilities in public places.

Arizona—

☞ Banned whites and blacks from marrying and threw in Mongolians, Malays, and Hindus as bad partners for whites, to boot. Wyoming did, too, adding mulattos.

Florida—

☞ Prohibited marriage to a white person for anyone of Negro descent to the fourth generation.

☞ Made the cohabitation of whites and blacks punishable by imprisonment for a year and a fine of $500.

☞ Mandated separate black and white schools.

Georgia—

☞ Banned black and white mental patients from occupying the same facilities.

☞ Barred blacks from acting as a barber to white women and girls.

☞ Barred white and black amateur baseball teams from playing within two blocks of each other.

☞ Banned whites from selling wine to people of different races in the same room.

Kentucky—

☞ Barred white and black juvenile delinquents from occupying the same buildings.

Louisiana—

☞ Mandated that circuses provide separate entrances and ticket-selling areas for whites and blacks.

☞ Banned landlords from renting their property to whites and blacks at the same time.

☞ Mandated separate facilities for white and black blind persons.

Mississippi—

☞ Prohibited every person from advancing the concept of social equality or intermarriage between blacks and whites, upon pain of six months in jail and a $500 fine.

North Carolina—

☞ Barred whites and blacks from trading textbooks from year to year, requiring instead that once a race started using a book, only that race could ever have that book.

Oklahoma—

☞ Barred whites and blacks from fishing, boating, or bathing together.

☞ Mandated separate telephone booths for whites and blacks.

Virginia—

☞   Required whites and blacks to attend the theater separately.[21]

The Mississippi Vagrant Act of 1865 provided: "that all freedmen, free negroes, and mulattoes in this State, over the age of eighteen years, found on the second Monday in January, 1866, or thereafter, with no lawful employment or business, or found unlawfully assembling themselves together, either in the day or night time…shall be deemed vagrants, and on conviction thereof shall be fined in the sum of not exceeding fifty dollars…and imprisoned, at the discretion of the court…not exceeding ten days." And, *An Act to Confer Civil Rights on Freedmen, and for other Purposes* stated: "Every civil officer shall, and every person may, arrest and carry back to his or her legal employer any freedman, free negro, or mulatto who shall have quit the service of his or her employer before the expiration of his or her term of service without good cause…" Mississippi Black Code, 1865.[22]

Thus, did the States' Rights crowd continue slavery through the enactment of state laws, even after its legal abolishment in the United States. In 1866, Florida passed *An Act Prescribing Additional Penalties For The Commission Of Offenses Against The State*, making it "…unlawful for any negro, mulatto, or other person of color, to own, use, or keep in his possession or under his control any bowie-knife, dirk, sword, fire-arms, or ammunition of any kind, unless he first obtain a license to do so from the judge of probate of the county in which he may be a resident for the time being…" States' Rights proponents ardently protect the American right to keep and bear arms, yet took even that right away from African-Americans.

Most distressing of all, the lynching of African-American men became a favorite Southern pastime. Between 1889 and 1930 alone, nearly 3,000 African-Americans were lynched in the United States.[23] In the face of these discriminatory laws and the physical atrocities perpetrated against them, perhaps African-Americans would have been justified with their own Bunker Hills.

---

21. "Jim Crow Laws," *Martin Luther King, Jr., National Historic Site,* at http://www.nps.gov/malu/documents/jim_crow_laws.htm
22. "Mississippi Black Codes," *What You Need To Know About,* at http://afroamhistory.about.com/library/blmississippi_blackcodes.htm
23. "Lynching, Education on the Internet & Teaching History Online," http://www.spartacus.schoolnet.co.uk/USAlynching.htm

Instead, white America owes African-Americans a large debt of gratitude for putting up with the "legal" discrimination and violence as long as they did and for working within our flawed system to greatly improve it.

In truth, the country failed to heal the wounds between black and white during the period known as "Reconstruction." The story of this failure was fully set out in *Birth of a Nation*, the first epic film in history—and to this day a racist icon. *Birth of a Nation* was *Jurassic Park* and *Saving Private Ryan* all rolled into one. It had more impact on American thought than just about any book, and there was no real competition at the movies at the time. The movie is not about the *birth* of America, but about its supposed <u>re</u>-*birth* after the Civil War, and it presents the outrageous theme that America was not made whole until white Northerners joined white Southerners to establish Jim Crow in the South through the Ku Klux Klan. In fact, the movie ends with armed and mounted knights of the Ku Klux Klan keeping the black citizens of the South away from the polling places. That is the theme that helped to propel Hollywood, and it stayed in the white psyche for the entire 20th Century. In fact, it's still there.

Today's Conservatives carry on their tradition. Remember all of the tumult raised when then Senate Majority Leader Trent Lott spoke at (now late) Senator Strom Thurmond's 100th birthday in 2002? Lott bubbled over with praise, stating: "I want to say this about my state: When Strom Thurmond ran for President, we voted for him. We're proud of it. And, if the rest of the country had followed our lead, we wouldn't have had all these problems over all these years, either." Lott was the man the Republican party chose as its Senate Leader and who was, therefore, the face of the Republican party for most of the Clinton White House years.

Thurmond, the man whom Lott thought deserved such effusive praise, ran for President as the segregationist Dixiecrat candidate in 1948. The Dixiecrat platform supported the Conservative notions that white people and African-Americans should not ride on the bus together, eat together, play professional sports together, or stay in the same hotel together. Heaven forbid if they actually drank out of the same water cooler, or used the same bathroom.

Thurmond was a signer on to "The Southern Manifesto," presented to the United States Senate in 1956 by 19 Senators and 77 House Members from 11 states.[24] These 11 states were the same that made up the 11 states of the Confederacy. The Manifesto was issued in response to the Supreme Court's decision in *Brown v. Board of Education*, which led to the desegregation of public schools, by law if not by practice. The Manifesto proclaimed that:

> We regard the decisions of the Supreme Court in the school cases as a clear
> abuse of judicial power. It climaxes a trend in the Federal Judiciary under-
> taking to legislate, in derogation of the authority of Congress, and to
> encroach upon the reserved rights of the states and the people.
>
> The original Constitution does not mention education. Neither does the
> 14th Amendment nor any other amendment....
>
> When the amendment was adopted in 1868, there were 37 States of the
> Union...Every one of the 26 States that had any substantial racial differ-
> ences among its people, either approved the operation of segregated schools
> already in existence or subsequently established such schools by action of
> the law-making body which considered the 14th Amendment.
>
> In the case of *Plessy v. Ferguson* in 1896 the Supreme Court expressly
> declared that under the 14th Amendment no person was denied any of his
> rights if the States provided separate but equal facilities. This decision has
> been followed in many other cases. It is notable that the Supreme Court,
> speaking through Chief Justice Taft, a former President of the United
> States, unanimously declared in 1927 in *Lun v. Rice* that the "separate but
> equal" principle is "within the discretion of the State in regulating its public
> schools and does not conflict with the 14th Amendment."...
>
> This unwarranted exercise of power by the Court, contrary to the Constitu-
> tion, is creating chaos and confusion in the States principally affected. It is
> destroying the amicable relations between white and Negro races that have
> been created through 90 years of patient effort by the good people of both
> races. It has planted hatred and suspicion where there has been heretofore
> friendship and understanding...
>
> Even though we constitute a minority in the present Congress, we have full
> faith that a majority of the American people believe in the dual system of
> government which has enabled us to achieve our greatness and will in time
> demand that the reserved rights of the States and of the people be made
> secure against judicial usurpation.[25]

Like Calhoun's report that some Senators believed that "the agitation"
about slavery would break apart the Union because it trampled on States'

---

24. *The Congressional Record*, 84th Congress Second Session, Vol. 102, part
4 (Washington: Governmental Printing Office, 1956), 4459-4460.
25. *Ibid.*, 4459-4460.

Rights, Thurmond and the other Manifesto supporters signed on to the theory that interracial schooling would have the same effect—"destroying the amicable relations" of the races that were 90 years in the making of "friendship and understanding," because it also destroyed States' Rights. Forty-six years later, Senator Lott and his party were still preaching identical racist nonsense. And, don't forget the lynchings.

Indeed, Thurmond took the same view of the Civil War as did Calhoun. As noted by author Joseph Martin Hernon, in supporting the Dred Scot decision, a pre-Civil War ruling by the Supreme Court that mandated the return of runaway slaves to the South, Thurmond argued:

> "The war between the States was brought on because the social revolutionaries refused to stop at the Constitutional barrier cited by the Supreme Court." After the Civil War, in his view, the Fourteenth Amendment was "legislated and imposed by force of arms...to preserve the appearance of legality." The *Brown* decision of the Supreme Court in 1954 revealed that the "intent of the Framers of the Constitution and previous judicial decisions could be ignored.[26]

This sort of legalistically cloaked racism also received strong support from the nascent modern conservative movement led by people such as William F. Buckley, Jr., a man who, in Ronald Reagan's words, "changed our country...indeed our century."[27] Buckley founded *National Review* Magazine to trumpet the Conservative philosophy. Initially published in 1955, *National Review* tried at first to make the same tired States' Rights "Constitutional" arguments against desegregating the public schools, but Buckley wrote an editorial in August 1957 that took the sheep's clothing off the wolf:

> The central question that emerges...is whether the white community in the South is entitled to take such measures as are necessary to prevail, politically and culturally, in areas in which it does not dominate numerically. The sobering answer is *Yes*—the white community is so entitled because, for the time being, it is the advanced race.... the question, as far as the white community is concerned, is whether the claims of civilization super-

---

26. Joseph Martin Hernon, *Profiles in Character, Hubris and Heroism in the U.S. Senate 1789–1990* (New York: M.E. Sharpe Armonk, 1997), 194.
27. John B. Judis, *William F. Buckley, Jr., Patron Saint of the Conservatives* (New York: Simon and Schuster, 1988), inside dust-cover.

cede those of universal suffrage.... *National Review* believes that the South's premises are correct.[28]

Such a proposition is not surprising from a man who wrote in his best-selling book, *Up From Liberalism*, "My own notion, for instance, is that the Jewish race can probably be demonstrated to be more intelligent than the Gentile, on the average; as Gentiles might be shown to be superior to Negroes in intelligence."[29]

As the 1960s began, Buckley tried to back off this type of race-based defense for segregation, returning instead to the coded message of States' Rights, and, according to his biographer, John B. Judis, "[i]nsisting that the federal imposition of integration was a greater evil than the temporary continuation of segregation."[30] Buckley rationalized, "If it is true that the separation of the races on account of color is nonrational, then circumstance will in due course break down segregation."[31] That means that after almost 200 years of the "States' Rights" charade and one Civil War fought to end it, the Conservatives still tried to sell America on the idea that racial discrimination was a "temporary" condition that would break down "in due course." Buckley even defended Mississippi Governor Ross Barnett's right to exclude African-American students at the University of Mississippi in 1962.[32] Buckley had not changed by 1967 when, in his August 19 column for *National Review*, he lumped together Hitler, Lenin, and Martin Luther King, writing:

> Repression is an unpleasant instrument, but it is absolutely necessary for civilizations that believe in order and human rights. I wish to God Hitler and Lenin had been repressed. And word should be gently got through to the non-violent avenger Dr. King, that in the unlikely event that he succeeds in mobilizing his legions, they will be most efficiently, indeed most zestfully, repressed.[33]

Moreover, Buckley's *Up From Liberalism* aptly demonstrates that Conservative racism is inherently anti-democratic. The first racist thing about that

---

28. *Ibid.*, 138-139.
29. *Ibid.*, 192.
30. *Ibid.*, 192.
31. *Ibid.*, 192.
32. *Ibid.*, 192-193.
33. *Ibid.*, 269.

book is its title, a parody on the Booker T. Washington autobiography *Up From Slavery*. Using an African-American's book title to promote racism is racist in itself. In addition, *Up From Liberalism* argues that democracy is not necessarily a good thing, because it can land power in the hands of black people, either here or in Africa:

> In *Up From Liberalism*, Buckley argued that the Liberal preoccupation with the method of politics—democracy—was justifying the enlargement of government power at the expense of individual freedoms and states' rights. Liberals, he charged, had mistaken a mere means to a just, virtuous, and harmonious society for an end in itself. Echoing Frank Meyer, Buckley wrote:
>
> > The democracy of universal suffrage is not a bad form of government; it is simply not necessarily nor inevitably a good form of government. Democracy must be justified by its works, not doctrinaire affirmations of an intrinsic goodness that no mere method can legitimately lay claim to.
>
> Buckley gave two examples of how this obsession with democracy warped the liberals' judgment. In the white South, he contended, liberals who pursued "the absolute right of universal suffrage" for the Negro were endangering existing standards of civilization, which were maintained by the superior "cultural advancement" of the white community. And in Africa, by acceding to black demands for independence and "one man, one vote," whites were inviting a return to barbarism:
>
> > We see in the revolt of the masses in Africa the mischief of the white man's abstractions: for the West has, by its doctrinaire approval of democracy, deprived itself of the moral base from which to talk back to the apologists of rampant nationalism. The obvious answer to a Tom Mboya [the Kenyan nationalist] is: Your people sir, are not ready to rule themselves.[34]

While Buckley wrote the proven truth that democracy does not guarantee good government—Hitler was democratically elected—Buckley's choice of "evidence" to support this truth only revealed Conservatism's racist foundation. White culture in the American South was superior, Buckley wrote, and permitting black people in Africa to vote would return that continent to barbarism. The Conservatives' "intellectual champion" was telling African-Americans to keep their place. Ironically, Kenya is now a key United States ally and

---

34. *Ibid.*, 168-169

a pretty successful democracy, albeit with problems to overcome. And it is certain that Europe's theft of African natural resources and Europe's initial institution of African governments meant to serve their European masters, rather than their own people, has something to do with Africa's continuing problems.

Strom Thurmond, of course, opposed both the Civil Rights law of 1964 and the Voting Rights Act of 1965. Conservatives considered the Voting Rights Act a wild piece of legislation, in that its primary purpose was to ensure: "No voting qualification or prerequisite shall be imposed or applied by any State or political subdivision to deny or abridge the right of any citizen of the United States to vote on account of race or color." By opposing the Voting Rights Act, Conservatives implicitly conceded that their so-called "literacy" tests and "good moral character" tests as prerequisites to voting were no such thing, but were merely intended to keep minorities from voting. Thurmond was also given veto power over Richard Nixon's choice for his vice-presidential running mate in 1968, and he coronated Conservative liberal-bater Spiro Agnew rather than moderate Senator John A. Volpe from Massachusetts.[35]

How very unfortunate that we did not elect Senator Thurmond President, so that "we wouldn't have had all these problems over all these years." Sadly, from the Constitution's "60 percent" rule, to Calhoun, to Davis, to Thurmond, to Lott, the Conservatives have been singing the same tune of States' Rights as *the* supporting foundation for advancing racism over the course of more than 225 years of American history.

The most bizarre thing about the whole ugly and profound Thurmond influence upon Conservative thinking is an item confirmed in December 2003, but first rumored long before then: Thurmond fathered a mixed race daughter, Essie Mae Washington-Williams.[36]

Thurmond's daughter was born when he was 22 to his former maid, who was all of 16 years old. Depending on the daughter's birthday, the mother may well have been only 15 when the child was conceived. Against the background of the Jim Crow South, and because neither Thurmond nor the mother of his daughter is alive, the question of whether the relationship between the maid

---

35. Hernon, 195.
36. Michael Janofsky, "Segregationist's family admits mixed race child," *The New York Times* and others, December 17, 2003.

and Thurmond was voluntary cannot be determined. However, whether or not there was any wrong on Thurmond's part in the conception of the child, there was great societal wrong in his and others' treatment of his daughter, notwithstanding her own opinion that she is proud to be her father's child.

Thurmond's Conservative colleagues covered up this chapter of his life, even after attending his funeral, but let him prattle on for more than *50 years* on the public scene as a racist, whether overt or covert. Onto the basically agreeable propositions that people should rely upon themselves first and government second, the Conservatives have grafted a diabolically dangerous, venomously venial, maladroitly malignant hatred of other races. Not only has this racism caused the death of millions—slave master and bonds-breaker alike—and the death and maiming of tens of thousands or more through lynching and beatings, it also has resulted in lasting degradation and harm to the victims of Jim Crow and our society as a whole. Yet it consistently has been dressed up as a respectable part of the debate even by those who, like Thurmond, would have their own children forced by police to ride in the back of the bus and live in shacks so that they themselves could ride in the front and live in mansions!

This racism is behind the Conservatives' whole masquerade. Conservatives who are truly non-racist must come to grips with the fact that monied and propertied Conservatives have spread this politically malevolent virus throughout our land for their own purposes. If you allow the virus to infect you by siding with them in our great national debate, you are either a carrier or have an active case of their disease.

The lengths to which Conservatives will go to defend even the overt racists among them is at times amusing. Francophile (in the sense of Francisco, not Paris) columnist and talking-head Ann Coulter even tried to blame Liberals for Thurmond, through the faulty syllogism Democrat = Liberal. Coulter writes:

> What the Lott incident shows is that Republicans have to be careful about letting Democrats into our party. Back when they supported segregation, Lott and Thurmond were Democrats. This is something the media are intentionally hiding to make it look like the Republican Party is the party of segregation and race discrimination, which it never has been.
>
> In 1948, Thurmond did not run as a "Dixiecan," he ran as a "Dixiecrat"—his party was an offshoot of the Democratic Party. And when he lost, he went right back to being a Democrat. This whole brouhaha is about

a former Democrat praising another former Democrat for what was once a Democrat policy.[37]

Although most Liberals are Democrats and most Conservatives are Republicans, neither is universally so. Coulter's backhanded attempt to brand Liberals as racists, by noting that Thurmond and Lott are former Democrats, is intellectually dishonest, because she knows that the common threads to their party affiliation are race and Conservatism, which they carried with them in both parties. In 2004, it is Coulter and the Conservatives, not Liberals, who defended Thurmond.

On her website, Coulter continues her intellectual dishonesty by calling Liberals racists—against white people, no less:

> Republicans made Southern Democrats drop the race nonsense when they entered the Republican Party. Democrats supported race discrimination, then for about three years they didn't, now they do again. They've just changed which race they think should be discriminated against.[38]

Coulter seems to be attacking affirmative action. Even assuming the extreme position that all affirmative action is objectionably discriminatory, when a writer throws upon one side of the scale the horrors of slavery—from the capture of human beings in Africa to their inhuman transport to our shores to their chains and brands and the raping of women, the break-up of their families, the enforced labor, and the inadequate food and shelter—together with the history of Jim Crow, the lynchings, the job and housing discrimination, and the denial of civil rights such as voting, and loads onto the other side of the scale whether some white kid has to go to the University of Iowa instead of the University of Michigan, and then equates them, as Coulter's argument essentially does, well, only a writer trying to justify racism would do that.

Coulter's website further launches into a diatribe that leaves the not-so-subtle impression that Henry Wallace, another breakaway Democrat who received about a million votes in 1948 when Thurmond ran for President, was a leftist Democrat, and all Democrats must be like him. Next, she decides that

---

37. Ann Coulter, "Democrats: A Lott of Trouble," December 18, 2002, at http://www.anncoulter.com/columns/2002/121802.htm
38. *ibid.*

Henry Wallace was really a communist, so all modern Liberals, who are Democrats like Wallace, must therefore be communists.[39] Thus, Coulter employs the age-old device of changing the subject when wrong.

In the early 1960s, George Corley Wallace, the late governor of Alabama who defied the mandate of a Federal Court to integrate the University of Alabama by standing in the way of the first African-Americans to enroll there, helped to launch the modern Conservative movement by couching racism in a States' Rights philosophy. He is quoted as saying:

> Today I have stood where Jefferson Davis stood and took an oath to my people. It is very appropriate then that from this Cradle of the Confederacy, this very heart of the great Anglo-Saxon Southland, that today we sound the drum for freedom...Let us rise to the call of freedom-loving blood that is in us and send our answer to the tyranny that clanks its chains upon the South. In the name of the greatest people that ever trod this earth, I draw the line in the dust and toss the gauntlet before the feet of tyranny, and I say: segregation now, segregation tomorrow, segregation forever...Government has become our god. It is a system that is the very opposite of Christ. The international racism of the liberals seeks to persecute the international white minority to the whim of the international colored so that we are footballed about according to the favor of the Afro-Asian bloc...[If the races] amalgamate into the one unit as advocated by the Communist philosopher, then we become a mongrel unit of one under a single, all-powerful government...We invite the Negro citizen of Alabama to work with us from his separate racial station to grow in individual freedom and enrichment...But we warn those of any group who would follow the false doctrines of communistic amalgamation that we will not surrender our system of government, or freedom of race and religion [that] was won at a hard price; and if it requires a hard price to retain it, we are able—and quite willing—to pay it.[40]

We Liberals have to be educated. We never realized that the "freedom of race" was a right guaranteed by the Constitution.

As the Democratic Party took Hubert Humphrey's advice and moved out of the shadow of States' Rights and into the sunshine of civil rights, the Conservatives saw a chance to make hay from racism by jumping to the Republi-

---

39. *Ibid.*
40. Bruun and Crosby, 729-730.

can Party. An internet account of this traces the origin to the Presidential campaign of Barry Goldwater:

> Arizona senator Barry Goldwater began the Republicans' catering to Southern racism in his 1964 presidential race against Lyndon Johnson. Realizing a large share of the black vote was going to Johnson, who was working on crafting the landmark 1964 Civil Rights Act, Goldwater came out against it, and went for states' rights instead. This helped him ride the wave of white backlash, and he carried the five Deep South (Dixiecrat) states of Louisiana, Mississippi, Alabama, Georgia and South Carolina. This was unheard of for a Republican at the time.[41]

Yet Goldwater appears to have been personally free of racial prejudice, according to one of his biographers:

> Goldwater was a foe of all forms of discrimination, and despite his opposition to the Civil Rights Act of 1964 on clearly defined constitutional grounds, this was his strong personal commitment. His lifelong actions and leadership in fighting and ending discrimination went far beyond typical, often hypocritical political rhetoric. In 1946, he provided for the first desegregated unit during the organization of the Arizona Air National Guard. That was two decades before the 1964 Civil Rights Bill. He was a longtime supporter of both the NAACP and the Urban League in Phoenix. And he insisted on desegregating the Goldwater's stores soon after he went to work there in his early twenties. "Never in my life," he said with passion, "had I ever advocated, suggested, or implied any form of racism."[42]

Nevertheless, Goldwater's strategy of bringing the South into the Republican Party may have been farsighted (it certainly didn't help his own campaign), but it necessarily played upon, and ultimately made the Republican party a victim of, old-fashioned racism.

In the presidential election that followed, Richard Nixon carried forward with Goldwater's strategy, according to the same report on *Alternet*:

---

41. Lee Hubbard, "Does the GOP Have Racial Amnesia?" Alternet, March 20, 2001, at http://www.alternet.org/story.html?StoryID=10614
42. Bill Rentschler, *Goldwater, A Tribute to a Twentieth-Century Political Icon* (Lincolnwood, Illinois: Contemporary Books, 2000), 190-191.

Richard Nixon's "Southern strategy" used tactics from the Goldwater and Dixiecrat playbook of George Wallace to play on white fear and resentment by labeling blacks "welfare cheats" and "laggards." The white backlash to the Civil Rights Movement and to LBJ's Great Society programs (which, paradoxically, gave poor Southern white people unprecedented access to health care, education, and job training) helped elect Nixon, and the party wrote off black voters completely.[43]

After taking a headcount, these Republicans concluded that their traditional trampling of minority rights would actually pay political dividends. The report further states:

> "Substantial Negro support is not necessary to national Republican victory," said Kevin Phillips, the mastermind behind the Nixon strategy. "The GOP can build a winning coalition without Negro votes. Indeed, Negro-Democratic mutual identification was a major source of Democratic loss and Republican party profit in many sections of the country."[44]

Professor Friedrich von Hayek, a Conservative icon who posits that capitalism is a necessary, if not sufficient, basis for freedom, has written eloquently about the dangers of concentrating power in a strong central government.[45] But von Hayek was an Austrian, well-acquainted with Hitler's "aunschloss" of his native country and the horrors of Nazism. Certainly, if I lived in Germany, I would be a diehard federalist and "States' Righter." The central government is the Germans' enemy because, historically, whenever it has united the German states and principalities—whether under Bismarck, Kaiser Wilhelm II, or der Fuhrer—disaster has befallen the country and/or its neighbors as it murders all those in its way. But, in our country, the situation is exactly the opposite. Here, "States' Rights" is decidedly not an academic discussion over the pros and cons of a "federalist" system of government. Any such discussion misses the entire point of American history. Federalism has its good points, but in the life of the United States of America, the devolution of power from Washington has meant one thing and one thing only—oppression and racism.

---

43. Hubbard, at http://www.alternet.org/story.html?StoryID=10614
44. *Ibid.*
45. *See* Friedrich von Hayek, *The Road To Serfdom* (Chicago: University of Chicago Press, 1944).

Right-thinking people must stand with Lincoln and his descendants, not Davis and his. The *Alternet* story continues:

> Since then, some Republicans across the country have played to these fears to gather white votes. Ronald Reagan declared that he "believed in states' rights" when he kicked off a presidential campaign in Philadelphia, Mississippi, where civil rights martyrs Schwerner, Chaney and Goodman were murdered, fighting States' Rights and attempting to help blacks get registered to vote. Once in office, Reagan used the racialized image of "welfare queens" who drive Cadillacs, and he led an all out assault on affirmative action laws by calling them "reverse racism."[46]

The racist States' Rights philosophy lived on through Thurmond who, after Reagan's election, was on the Board of Trustees of Bob Jones University when the school was given a tax break with Reagan's support. Bob Jones University barred interracial dating and marriage. Presidents George Bush and George W. Bush also are supporters of Bob Jones University; the younger George Bush made a point of campaigning there in the 2000 Presidential campaign. And, even though he likely would have beaten Michael Dukakis handily anyway, George the 41st could not resist running his "Willie Horton" ads, which blandished a scary-looking African-American's face across all America's television screens, and not very subtly implied that all African-Americans are criminals.

The same ode to States' Rights plays on as a key instrument in the Conservative symphony orchestra. In the fall of 1999, as the Republican primary season started to gather steam for the following year's national election, the candidates took positions on whether the Confederate battle flag's "stars and bars" should be eliminated from South Carolina's own state flag. Then a mere candidate for the Republican nomination, George W. Bush appeared at a rally in Simpsonville, South Carolina, and offered, "My advice is for people who don't live in South Carolina to butt out of the issue. The people of South Carolina can make that decision."[47] Oh, no, they can't—any more than they could make the right decision about slavery, the Black Codes, the Ku Klux Klan, Jim Crow, or whether to support the "Southern Manifesto" or the Civil

---

46. Hubbard, at http://www.alternet.org/story.html?StoryID=10614
47. Leigh Strope, "Bush dismissive of NAACP push on Confederate flag issue," *Associated Press*, September 7, 1999.

Rights revolution of the 1960s. The people of South Carolina boast a 100% failure rate in matters of this kind, and it was up to all who believe the right side won in 1865 to come to grips with those failures.

The performance of then Republican rival to Bush, Senator John McCain, was in some ways worse. McCain said of the flag, "I believe it's a symbol of heritage."[48] Well, it *is* a symbol of heritage—in the same way that the bodies left behind by Dillinger were a symbol of a certain independent streak. At least McCain later confessed that he was only pandering for votes when he made his comment.[49] It is evident that even in 2000 and beyond, any candidate who wants to win the Republican nomination, which goes through South Carolina, and who wants to prevail in the fall general election, which goes through the South (those Red States!) must still play the States' Rights card. Bush's phrasing—"the people of South Carolina can make that decision"—is a perfect example of his playing the race card.

He used it to gain the support of the living Confederates. One of the leading living Confederates in South Carolina is Richard Hines, described by Princeton professor Sean Wilentz:

> Hines first gained national media attention in 1996 when, in a public protest over the unveiling of a monument to the black tennis great Arthur Ashe in Richmond, Va., he unfurled the battle flag of his great-grandfather's [Confederate] regiment and denounced the statue as "a sharp stick in the eye of those who honor the Confederate heritage." By the time of the Ashe incident, Hines had been involved in neo-Confederate activities for well over a decade, as an activist in the *Sons of Confederate Veterans* and, even more flamboyantly, as managing editor of and contributor to the notorious pro-slavery magazine *Southern Partisan*. (Among his essays for the magazine was an effusive 1984 eulogy to Preston Brooks, the secessionist South Carolina representative best-known for his almost lethal caning of anti-slavery Sen. Charles Sumner on the Senate floor in 1856.)[50]

---

48. "Candidates battle over Confederate flag ahead of S.C. protest," *CNN online*, January 17, 2000, at http://www.cnn.com/2000/ALLPOLI-TICS/stories/01/17/s.carolina.flag/index.html

49. Steven A. Holmes, "McCain Admits He Wasn't Candid on Confederate Flag Issue," *New York Times*, April 20, 2000, republished by Congressman Jesse Jackson, Jr. (D.Ill.), at http://www.jessejacksonjr.com/issues/i042000146.html

As the Bush-McCain battle drew to a close, Hines paid for the mass mailing of more than 250,000 letters praising Bush for his flag stance while finding McCain's stance wanting.[51] Professor Wilentz also notes that John Ashcroft, the Bush administration's Attorney General, gave an interview to the Hines-related *Southern Partisan* magazine. In that interview, he praised the magazine for helping to "set the record straight" and for "defending Southern patriots like [Robert E.] Lee, [Thomas "Stonewall"] Jackson, and [Jefferson] Davis."[52] Thus, in a White House controlled by the party of Lincoln, at least in name, the Attorney General is a fan of the racists and secessionists implacably opposed by Lincoln.

Others at the top of the Conservative cause continue on with their traditional battle against minorities. Until recently, Trent Lott was a frequent speaker at events hosted by the St. Louis-based Council of Conservative Citizens (CCC), described by the Anti-Defamation League (ADL) as tracing its roots "directly to the racist, anti-integrationist White Citizens' Councils of the 1950s and 1960s. Its current leader, attorney Gordon Lee Baum, was an organizer for the WCC and built Citizens in part from the old group's mailing lists."[53]

There's a commonality in pronouncing the sounds of "KKK" and "CCC." Perhaps the CCC would point out that the last "C" is soft. I don't know, but I'd be interested to see what CCC members say on this point after a martini or two.

Conservatives remain enamored of racism. Just take a look at the October 16, 2003, web page for the Council of Conservative Citizens.[54] Among the readings are "Steele: In Defense of Racism," "*Angry White Female:* Walking While White," and The Racial Compact." Quirky anti-semitism is covered with "Did Rothschild Write *The Protocols?*" by someone named Macow. A

---

50. Sean Wilentz, "Inveterate Confederates: The southern skeletons in the Bush administration's closet," *The American Prospect*, at http://www.prospect.org/print-friendly/webfeatures/2002/12/wilentz-s-12-20.html
51. *Ibid.*
52. *Ibid.*
53. Anti-Defamation League Law Enforcement Agency Resource Network, http://www.adl.org/learn/Ext_US/CCCitzens.asp?xpicked=3&item=12
54. *Council of Conservative Citizens*, http://www.cofcc.org

picture of that learned treatise, "*The King Holiday and Its Meaning*," invites readers to "click on the image above to buy the book which reveals the TRUTH about Martin Luther King and why he does not deserve a national holiday in his honor." (Take that, Liberals!)

At the CCC's news website, editor Beauregarde (the name of a Confederate General) writes about important issues of the day, noting, "Britney Spears is the product of a conservative Southern family who was enrolled in an all-white private academy in Mississippi to avoid the very mischief she now wallows in."[55] This type of comment shows two things. First, white people can wallow on their own as well as any others. Second, Conservatives still believe that "race-mixing" leads to wallowing.

If we could just slough this off as the raving of a few political lunatics, that would be one thing. But full display is given to the picture of six prominent white men with a caption that says: "The election year Mississippi *Black Hawk Barbecue and Rally* held on July 19 drew dozens of political candidates attended by a crowd of over 500. The Black Hawk Barbeque is sponsored by the *Council of Conservative Citizens* to raise money for private academy school buses...." Those pictured include Mississippi State Senator Bucky Huggins, and more important, "gubernatorial nominee Haley Barbour"!

Haley Barbour did not just run and win his campaign for Governor of Mississippi; he also was and remains Chairman of the Republican *National* Committee. As recently as January 29, 2004, Barbour attended a meeting of the RNC where, according to *The New York Times*, "The strategy part of the session was left to" him.[56] So what does this very important politician stand for? Well, Barbour's website features a big picture of the Mississippi State Capital with Old Glory faded into the background, while the Mississippi state flag, very bright, waves in the wind, so as best to draw attention to itself and to its most prominent part—you guessed it—the Confederate battle flag.[57] True then, it is, that for the past decade, the Conservatives were led at both their National Committee and in the United States Senate itself, by active CCC-supporting sons of Jefferson Davis. The Confederates have now taken over as the architects of the whole party.

55. http://www.cofcc.org/news.htm
56. "Republicans Attack Kerry at Party Meeting," *The New York Times*, January 30, 2004
57. http://www.haleybarbour.com

These examples from the past 214 years, including even these most recent examples, show that Conservatives are simply unfit for public office and will remain so ever more while this type of racist pandering, which has always been at the heart of their movement, continues. Although he was speaking positively, Jesse Jackson once pointed out something to a small group of people of which I was part that makes this Conservative refusal to do away with its racism so much more distressing than it would be ordinarily. Jackson noted that the people who have most benefitted from the end of Jim Crow are *white* people. If this country had stayed Jim Crow, there would be no Atlanta Braves, no Houston Astros, no gleaming Southern office buildings, and certainly there would have been no Atlanta Olympics. The African-Americans of this country forced the white South to get rich, yet white Conservatives still send their kids to private schools and complain about "big Washington government."

No Reparations For Slavery, But Damages For Jim Crow

One of the hottest issues on the talk show agenda, although many whites don't take it seriously or are even offended by it, is the question of whether African-Americans should receive "reparations" for slavery the way concentration camp survivors received reparations from the German government following the Second World War. Realizing the marked deck that white America has used while playing against them for the past 400 years, African-Americans support this idea. Representative John Conyers (D.Mich.) introduced in January 1989 Bill H.R. 40, Commission to Study Reparation Proposals for African Americans Act. A CNN/USA Today/Gallup poll showed that among black respondents, 55 percent said the government should make cash payments for reparations.[58]

While victims of slavery should have received recompense directly after the Civil War, the idea of paying reparations today is anachronistic and divisive. It serves only to undermine the Liberal cause, because it makes white Conservatives feel defensive while at the same time allowing them to refuse even to engage in a real debate over the issue. They enslaved no one, they can maintain, and no one who was a slave is still among us to receive the redress. In the spirit of not visiting the sins of the parents on the children, Conservatives are right that they enslaved no one. To the extent that compensating the seventh or so generation after slavery makes no practical sense, the Conservatives are

---

58.   http://www.cnn.com/2002/LAW/03/26/slavery.reparations/index.html

also right that the unofficial statute of limitations was crossed some time ago. Liberalism risks losing support among moderates if the reparations issue remains on the table. Most Americans will simply not take the slavery issue seriously because it is too remote in time, and they cannot and will not draw the connection between a slave in America and a present day, actually living African-American. Good movies have a shelf life of about 15 minutes, so Americans are not about to stop and contemplate what should be done about the distant descendants of people who were wronged by other people between 150 and 400 years ago. It just won't happen.

A three-pronged approach can resolve the reparations argument:

- Permit *living* African-Americans who have suffered direct, personal harm due to Jim Crow to be compensated—both those who lived in our apartheid South and those who passed through it. This group of people grows smaller with each passing year. The advantage of compensating these people, who can demonstrate real legal damage in the form of the deprivation of the rights guaranteed to them under the 1st and 14th Amendments, among others, is that they can relate what they *personally* experienced. There will be no academic debate about the harm, because the witnesses can make the case for themselves. Let everyone from Ernie Banks to the anonymous freedom bus riders and plain, church-going, model citizens of that time speak the truth about what they suffered. These people's stories can still move this country, as they did in the 1960s to overthrow Jim Crow in the first place.

- Continue (or start, as the case may be) to address specific deficiencies left over as a result of slavery, such as inferior schools in African-American neighborhoods.

- Budget serious American dollars as part of a global campaign to stamp out slavery in the rest of the world. What better way to honor the victims of our own slavery than to use their memory to break the yoke of the current taskmasters?

The African-Americans who suffered through Jim Crow can never actually be made whole by money any more than money can compensate the victim of a painful assault and battery. Moreover, the country could never afford to give the victims of Jim Crow the large damages our law would allow if the case of each victim were fully tried in a court. Why, the country could not even afford the legal apparatus to hear all those cases. The huge amounts involved would cause a backlash of resentment that would not be conducive to racial reconciliation. Rather, the monetary aspects of this solution should be handled in a more or less "it's the thought that counts" manner (but as much as possible on the "more" side). Perhaps a trust fund could be established for an extra pension for these victims as they grow older, which time is soon upon us and has passed for many of them. No one who is too young to have lived through Jim Crow could receive anything, and the compensation would increase depending on whether the person had a single bad experience while passing through a Jim Crow state or was born and reared there in the face of daily hatred. The United States should also lead the world in establishing an enormous "freedom fund" to eliminate slavery from the earth. The particulars could be left to Congress, which will be dealing with *real living victims* of *ascertainable Constitutional violations*, not the distant image of someone's great-great-great-great-great grandparents, notwithstanding those ancestors' ordeals. Let's use the memory of their suffering to lessen today's, and to bring Americans of all races together to recognize past sins as a step to let freedom ring as far as we can. This is not asking too much. A rich, white, suburbanite deprived by law of the right to vote, the right to use any drinking fountain when thirsty, the right to stay in any hotel when tired, the right to go to a state university, and the right to marry a person of a different race, among other things, would sue for millions just for him or herself—and get it. Certainly, victims of Jim Crow should get *something* that neither is minuscule nor will break the bank.

Liberal Federalism

None of this means that States have no rights; we do, after all, have a mixed national and state form of government. Misused, abused, and as abusive as this system has been by States' Righters, states do have a proper role to play in a progressive society. Adam Cohen, writing in our country's leading newspaper, observes:

> Louis Brandeis wrote one of his most enduring opinions in a case about ice. The facts of *The New State Ice Company v. Liebmann*, a dispute between the state of Oklahoma and a renegade ice manufacturer, have long been forgotten. But Brandeis's dissent contains one of the most famous formulations in American law: that the states should be free to serve as "laboratories" of democracy.[59]

Brandeis went a necessary step further, making the point that states have the *duty* to serve as such laboratories:

> The Depression, he wrote, had caused "an emergency more serious than war." Since "economic and social sciences are largely uncharted seas," he argued, the rational way to advance society was through "experimentation," the same "process of trial and error" as in the physical sciences.[60]

Cohen's *New York Times* article urges Liberals to use states to foster such things as gay marriage in times like these, when the federal government is oppressive. But encouraging states to act to limit a too-powerful central government is precisely the argument that the States' Rights crowd has used to justify its atrocities on our society. Therefore, it must be applied judiciously. We'd do better to concentrate on the positive nature of the States' power in developing programs that advance the progressive agenda *because they have proved workable* in the states before coming to the fore of the national agenda.

If this were universally accepted as the proper role for states, both Liberals and Conservatives could be happy with it—Liberals, because state governments would be looking for ways to help those who need it, and Conservatives, because the programs would be the product of *competition* among the states to make the best programs at the cheapest price. The people, too, would benefit, because not only would they get their programs at a good price, but any program that did not work could more easily be jettisoned.

---

59. Adam Cohen, "Brandeis's Views on States' Rights, And Ice-Making, Have New Relevance," *The New York Times*, December 7, 2003.
60. *Ibid.*

Reason 2. Liberals Support the "Strict Construction" of a Liberal Constitution.

Conservatives' "official" position on the courts is that they want appointed to the bench jurists who will declare the law as it "is," rather than what it "should be." Under this maxim, the President should submit for approval only judges who will "strictly construe" the Constitution to make sure that the Framers' "original intent" continues to be served. This theory was stated succinctly by one Conservative writer in an article whose theme was that Supreme Court Justice Sandra Day O'Connor was getting wobbly in her Conservatism:

> The late U.S. Supreme Court Justice Joseph Story, one of the great writers on the U.S. Constitution, described the Constitution as the "deliberate will of the people" and said that when "it is constitutionally altered, then and not until then, are the judges at liberty to disregard its original injunctions." However, activist liberal justices have for years treated the Constitution as a "living document" that changes with the times, based on those justices' whims of the moment. In effect, such justices are altering or amending the Constitution when their decisions do not follow a strict construction approach. For example, the so-called "right of privacy" used to justify a number of decisions is nowhere to be found in the language of the Constitution. If such a right is not expressly set out in the Constitution, shouldn't it be created by the legislature and not the courts?[1]

---

1. Randall Nunn, "Strict Construction or Trendy Political Correctness?" *American Daily*, July 4, 2003, at http://www.americandaily.com/item/1134

Conservatives have been running for office by running against a "runaway" judiciary for years. Nixon put a lot of effort into this area. As in so many areas, however, the motivation for the Conservative position was not an ode to a pristine Constitution; rather, it was just another way to keep the old order between whites and African-Americans in place as long as possible. This is certainly how, and why, current Chief Justice of the United States Supreme Court William H. Rehnquist obtained his appointment to that august body. Nixon biographer Melvin Small writes:

> Nixon's other appointee, Rehnquist, whom he had labeled a "clown" on one occasion because of the undignified way he dressed, was the intellectually impressive chief of the Office of Legal Counsel in the Justice Department. From the Goldwater faction of the party, the forty-seven year old Rehnquist was a conservative law-and-order man who had opposed the Civil Rights Act and earlier had supported the restrictive housing covenants and approved of the Supreme Court's 1896 *Plessy v. Ferguson* decision upholding government-mandated school segregation.[2]

Such are the rewards for advocating that African-Americans cannot live in your neighborhood or go to your schools—merely as a matter of principle, of course. Moreover, a 1999 article reports:

> When *Brown vs. Board of Education* was being argued, a clerk to U.S. Supreme Court Justice Robert Jackson suggested that the court should rule against the plaintiffs in the landmark school desegregation case. While making the case for maintaining segregated schools, the clerk sent a memo to his boss saying, "It is about time the Court faced the fact that white people in the South don't like the colored people." That clerk was William Rehnquist, now chief justice of the United States Supreme Court.[3]

Ronald Reagan thoroughly believed in this judicial "philosophy" and carried it out in his appointments. Edwin Meese, Reagan's Attorney General, revealed this in a speech:

2.　Melvin Small, *The Presidency of Richard Nixon* (University Press of Kansas, 1999), 172

3.　George E. Curry and Trevor W. Coleman Emerge, "Special Report, Hijacking Justice," *Rat House Reality, Ratical Branch*, October 1999, at http://www.ratical.org/ratville/CAH/hijakjustice.html

In selecting judges, the administration established a rigorous process of interviews and background-checking…. In addition to the nominee's professional qualifications, the president instructed us to consider his judicial philosophy. He wanted to name judges who would look at the Constitution and statute law and expound their evident meaning, rather than using loopholes or convoluted logic to reach some preconceived conclusion…. Judges who interpret and don't make the law, judges who are not activist, avoiding penumbras and emanations to impose personal values…. For them, the question involved in judicial restraint was not—and it is not—will we have a liberal or conservative court?…The question was, and is, will we have government by the people? And this is why the principle of judicial restraint has had an honored place in our tradition.[4]

The most obvious example of such an appointment was Reagan's nomination of Antonin Scalia to the High Court. George Bush the elder held the same position, first as part of the Reagan administration and again during his own. After all, he nominated Clarence Thomas to his seat on the Supreme Court. Thomas is the affirmative-action educated Justice who does not believe in affirmative action now that he has his piece of the action. Conservatives are inimically opposed to all affirmative action, although it is also why Sandra Day O'Connor, who graduated from the same law school class as Chief Justice William Rehnquist, beat the 8 billion to 1 odds (not an exact number, but close enough) of landing on the (same) Supreme Court.[5] Conservatives oppose affirmative action in order to make this country safe for personal favoritism and nepotism.

George Bush the younger adhered to this line when he ran for President. In the first 2000 Presidential debate, Bush said:

Voters should assume that I have no litmus test on that issue or any other issue. But the voters will know I'll put competent judges on the bench, people who will strictly interpret the Constitution and

4.   Mickey G. Craig, "Defending the Reagan Legacy: Rejecting Revisionist History," *Ashbrook Center for Public Affairs at Ashland University*, at http://www.ashbrook.org/publicat/monos/craig/home.html#15
5.   Jerry Goldman, "William H. Rehnquist," *Oyez*, at http://www.oyez.org/oyez/resource/legal_entity/100/biography

will not use the bench to write social policy. And that's going to be a big difference between my opponent and me. I—I believe that—I believe that the judges ought not to take the place of the legislative branch of government, that they're appointed for life and that they ought to look at the Constitution as sacred. They—they shouldn't misuse their bench. I don't believe in liberal activist judges. I believe in—I believe in strict constructionists.[6]

When asked what kind of Supreme Court appointments could be expected from him, Bush mentioned Antonin Scalia and Clarence Thomas.

Ann Coulter puts the issue this way:

> Somewhat disappointingly, it's impossible for conservative judges to wreck the country for liberals like liberal judges wrecked it for [conservatives]. Liberals are just being hysterical when they moan about Roe vs. Wade and should be ignored. There is really no such thing as a judicial activist on the right since the whole point of being a strict constructionist is that you don't hallucinate when reading the Constitution—and the Constitution simply doesn't say anything at all about most things anyone could possibly care about. Conservatives always knew they had to win at the ballot box; liberals prefer to skip voting and win by judicial fiat.[7]

Supreme Court Justice Antonin Scalia declares the same thing:

> ...this [Supreme] Court has [assumed] the power, not merely to apply the Constitution but to expand it, imposing what it regards as useful "prophylactic" restrictions upon Congress and the States. That is an immense and frightening antidemocratic power, and it does not exist.[8]

---

6.   "2nd Presidential Debate of the 2000 Campaign," *The New York Times*, October 11, 2000, republished at http://home.earthlink.net/~karen20000/text/2000presdeb1.html

7.   Ann Coulter, "Eight more Clarence Thomases," February 9, 2001, *Universal Press Syndicate*, republished by *Conservative Forum*, at http://www.conservativeforum.org/quotelist.asp?SearchType=5&Interest=28

8.   Antonin Scalia, Dissenting opinion in *Dickerson v. United States*, June 16, 2000, republished by *Conservative Forum*, at http://www.conservativeforum.org/quotelist.asp?SearchType=5&Interest=28

I'm a lawyer, and for the most part, I agree with the general proposition that judges ought to declare the law, not make it. I have had to tolerate, and sometimes confront, many judges who ignored the law, and it is a galling experience. For the most part, however, neither Conservative nor Liberal judges ignore the law for so grandiose a purpose as that of changing the Constitution.

Rather, they ignore the law for two other main purposes—one noble, and one ignoble. The noble reason is that it is human nature to listen to the facts, decide what is fair in one's own mind, and then find law to apply to the facts, regardless of whether it is the correct law. When I am on the right side of the law, but a judge ignores the law or more often cites law that does not really apply to the case just because that judge wants to do what s/he thinks is right, I may be aggravated, but I understand. The ignoble reason is that all judges are politicians—the judiciary is a branch of government, after all—and judges have their personal agendas to fulfill as politicians. Sometimes that means horse-trading a decision with a colleague, making a decision in the hope of a higher appointment, pleasing the ward boss by making a decision in which the ward boss has an interest, or ensuring that one's favored Presidential candidate takes office and can appoint others to the bench who will in turn ensure that the President's agenda is not opposed by the judiciary. When such a decision is made, all I can repeat is what one of my partners once said to me: it creates a sinking feeling in your stomach that never goes away, because the decision is so anomalous to an experienced lawyer that the fix is obvious.

When Conservatives rail against "activist" judges who want to impose on the rest of the country their personal views of what the Constitution *should* say, rather than what is does say, they're often referring to one of several politically charged types of cases. The cases tend to have society owning up to past injustices, which offends people who innocently supported the injustice. For example:

- Cases involving participation in the customs of the surrounding environment. Most Southern whites at one time were brought up to think it was perfectly normal and legal to prohibit African-Americans from drinking at the same fountain as white people, and just as normal and legal to make African-American children go to "separate but equal" schools that were of course not equal at all.

- Cases involving the protection of the rights of the guilty to protect the rights of innocent, such as not allowing illegally obtained evidence to be used to convict a person of a crime. There is indisputably in such a situation a type of wrong to the victim and society that goes unredressed, even if it is for the greater good.

- Cases involving the preservation of what Liberals claim are inherent rights, and Conservatives claim are new rights, such as the right to an abortion or the rights of committed gay couples to receive the same benefits as married straight people.

The Conservative position on virtually every one of these issues comes up both legally wrong and morally wrong. In the moral sense, while there may be some independent philosophical merit to the Conservative position in a vacuum, United States history has not been written in a vacuum. That history places Conservatism on the wrong side of every social issue we have ever confronted from border to border and sea to shining sea—slavery, Jim Crow, trust-busting, Social Security, Medicare, the environment, unionization, you-name-it. We would still be ruled by a semi-feudal oligarchy of rich white men if Conservatism had its way. That oligarchy would be free, but no one else would be. In the legal sense, the Conservative position lost when the South lost the Civil War and, therefore, *there is no more "original intent."* There is only original intent *plus the intent of all the Constitution's Amendments,* including the post-Civil War Amendments that granted Congress the authority to pass legislation it thought necessary to carry out those Amendments' intent.

No lawyer likes going to court and meeting a judge who will not apply the law because of outside pressure or his or her own sense of what is fair. The public never even sees these millions of cuts inflicted upon our legal system on a daily basis, except as litigants or jurors. Lay people serving on juries often do the same thing when they engage in the practice of "jury nullification" and refuse to follow the legal instructions given to them because they do not think it would be just to do so.[9] To the extent that it has validity, the Conservatives' "strict construction" argument reflects the natural distaste of being subject to a judge who refuses to follow the law because of his or her own agenda.

We Liberals have to some extent created our own "strict construction" problem, because we have often stretched certain parts of the Constitution to reach what we think is a just result. My mother had a phrase to describe her many children's good times gone awry. When the crescendo of noise became too loud at a gathering of young people, or when the clock rang well past the departing hour, she would plaintively ask, "Do you have to run it into the ground?" We all knew then that we had crossed the line. Liberalism, not to mention my own profession, lawyering, suffers from the same problem.

Here is how it works, or rather doesn't work, in the legal system. A legislature passes a law. Someone breaks it and is punished. The next time someone breaks it, some lawyer says, "Yes, Judge, but..." and gets the client off the hook. This, "but" makes perfect sense as an exception to the rule and is accepted by society. The next violation is followed by a new "but" from a new lawyer, drawing on the exceptional quality of the first one, but expanding it. After a sufficient time passes, there is no longer any of the original rule of law that started the whole process—only the "buts" remain. This is all justified by the lawyers saying that conditions and laws have to change, or we would still be kneeling in front of some king and throwing clods of dirt at each other to signify we have just sold our houses (people who can neither read nor write being able to remember the clod-throwing), rather than accomplishing the same thing in the more civilized fashion of recording a deed. No one can contest the initial justification, which is self-evident. But, what happens in far too many cases, and in a hurried fashion, is that we become so interested in protecting a right that we try to protect every tiny facet of every right, bogging everything down and giving credence to minor claims and injuries that should be resolved either in clearly defined and carried-out law or outside the law entirely.

9.   In one sense, judges' applying their own sense of fairness in the face of the law has an honored tradition in our legal system. When the English King made a law, it had to be followed to the letter. A person's only real chance at obtaining some surcease from such law was the Church, or "Chancery" courts, which could override the King's law within certain boundaries, because their authority came from a higher source. The "certain boundaries" part is important, because the Chancery courts could not just do anything they wanted in the face of the King's law, but had to act within certain prescribed principles to limit that law.

Liberalism operates the same way. Discrimination is bad, and with the possible exception of those smallpox-laden blankets given to the Native Americans, African-Americans suffered the worst torment of anyone in this country. Having come to the sound conclusion that discrimination against African-Americans and other ethnic groups must be addressed, however, Liberalism tends to run it into the ground. Even the slightest slight becomes grounds for federal intervention. Liberals should rein in this natural inclination of their philosophy. First, larger grievances are devalued by the insistence upon redressing minor ones. Second, it gives Conservatives the opportunity to attack the fundamentally solid Liberal positions by pointing to extremes that caricature those positions. We should not give up ourselves in this way to the Conservatives, whose positions are fundamentally weak. For example, comedians poke fun at "Indians" who reject that geographically politically incorrect name in order to substitute the name of an Italian map maker.

One example of how Liberals have made this error is the way we went about justifying the wholly Constitutional and wholly worthy civil rights laws of the 1960s, which was to forget their basis in the human rights inherent in the 13th and 14th Amendments and base them instead upon other rather arcane and inapplicable provisions of the Constitution. For instance, in *Katzenbach v. McClung*, the Supreme Court upheld a portion of the 1964 Civil Rights law barring discrimination in restaurant service by finding that Congress correctly could conclude that by obtaining a good portion of their food for resale from out of state, the service significantly affected interstate commerce, a federal concern. This decision certainly had a good societal effect, and maybe a reasonable person could agree with the reasoning at a stretch, but the decision was basically dishonest. The Commerce Clause was not put into the Constitution as a civil rights guarantee. It is not only dishonest to turn it into that, but relegating civil rights issues to the level of interstate commerce is demeaning.

The question then becomes how to have courts both apply the law and foster a Liberal society. The answer is to understand that, as written and as modified by its Amendments, the Constitution is a facially liberal document, so all we have to do is read it, and apply what it says liberally. The Constitution is the *Liberal's* friend, not the Conservative's, and we should not be afraid of interpreting it as such. That will dispatch the Conservatives' "strict construction" argument, as well as their narrow vision of our governmental structure.

Regarding the Civil Rights Commerce Clause decision, then, the law would have had a more solid foundation—and it would have been more in step with the times and much simpler—if the Supreme Court had just said that discrimination at restaurants stripped the customers of their 14th Amendment right not to be deprived of their liberty, or denied them their 14th Amendment right to equal protection of the law to peacefully shop wherever other persons within the jurisdiction of the United States were allowed to shop, or deprived them of any number of other Constitutional guarantees. If the Court could not uphold the law on one of these legitimate bases, then it was time either for a new law or maybe for civil strife to effectuate the change politically, but it was not time to uphold the law on the basis that restaurant service discrimination violated the *Commerce Clause*. There is no reason to contrive the Constitution, because the Constitution is on the Liberals' side.

In a more recent example, the Massachusetts Supreme Court granted the right to same-sex marriage and ordered the Massachusetts Legislature to write a law providing for it. This has sent the Conservatives into a panic, because they do not like gay people, or if we take Jerry Falwell at face value and as speaking for his followers, they certainly don't like gay people's behavior. Whether it is the people or the behavior they dislike, many Conservatives believe that they cannot condone, and no government of theirs can accept, same-sex marriage without going to hell; they believe that if they pass legislation in favor of same-sex marriage, they will themselves come to occupy an even lower step in the Inferno.

The Massachusetts decision unnecessarily has given people like Ann Coulter the opportunity to attack Liberals as out of the mainstream and as advocates of legally frivolous positions. It has often been an honor in American history to stand out of the mainstream, because our mainstream has committed huge crimes to go along with its great successes. So, Coulter's criticism scores no points. On the legal issue, however, her criticism—though delivered maliciously and with a disrespect of its own for the law—must be upheld in result, though not for the reasons she gives. Coulter writes:

> But there is absolutely no excuse for the Massachusetts legislature's jumping when Massachusetts Supreme Court Chief Justice Margaret Marshall says "jump." Marshall, immigrant and wife of New York Times columnist Anthony Lewis, has recently proclaimed a right to gay marriage for all of Massachusetts. She has further demanded that the legislature rewrite the law in accordance with her wishes.[10]

Let's stop here just a second. Coulter, like Conservatives in general, wants to make a point. But, she feels, as do Conservatives in general, that she cannot make her point without an *ad hominem* (against the person, not the idea) attack on the decision. Therefore, she attacks Justice Marshall as an immigrant. This is disgusting for many reasons. First, Coulter evidently was a good student and knows what she is doing, so her personal attack must be deemed as having been delivered with malice. Second, by attacking Marshall as "a feriner," Coulter lowers herself to the bottom of the Conservative-nativist pit. I might remind everyone that Albert Einstein was an immigrant. General Pulaski helped win our revolution, and he wasn't born in Boise. Arnold Schwarzenegger went from Austrian body-builder to Governor of California. We all know the history of immigration in this country: without it, we never would have survived.

Coulter continues:

> Ms. Marshall has as much right to proclaim a right to gay marriage from the Massachusetts Supreme Court as I do to proclaim it from my column. The Massachusetts legislature ought to ignore the court's frivolous ruling—and cut the justices' salaries if they try it again.[11]

In making this argument, Coulter shows her keen ability to misrepresent an important fact. She makes it appear as though Justice Marshall ruled alone, when in fact a majority of the Justices on her Court had to agree. Coulter also shows a sharp disrespect for the law by advocating a cut in the Massachusetts Justices' salaries to "make" them change their decision. Coulter, who professes to be a Constitutional scholar, should be aware at least as far as our full federal judges go (Marshall is a State Court judge), the very Constitution that Coulter claims to defend makes it illegal for Congress to lower their salaries to intimidate them. By advocating the salary cut in Massachusetts, Coulter demonstrates that she really does not trust the Constitutional principles she is trying to convince us are so important.

Putting aside her nativism, her misrepresentation by omission, and her disrespect for the Constitution, however, Coulter is right in her strictly legal

---

10. Ann Coulter, "Supreme Court Opinions Not Private Enough," December 4, 2003, *Human Events Online*, at http://www. humaneventsonline.com/article.php?id=2533

11. *Ibid.*

argument that the Massachusetts Supreme Court cannot tell the Massachusetts Legislature to define marriage one way or the other. Prior to any legislation under English law, there existed what is known as "the common law," which amounted to the customs of the people before the King got involved. Under the common law, people could get married without the usual solemnization—no service, either religious or civil—followed by cohabitation. The people had to be qualified to marry, however, and this meant one man and one woman. That's the system that was passed to America by the English colonists and made part of our law.

However, in many American jurisdictions, including my own state of Illinois, common law marriage was banned. Marriage came under the purview of the Illinois Legislature, so that even a man and a woman who considered themselves married, had 15 children together, celebrated their "anniversary," and cohabited for their entire lives were *not* considered married. That could have serious legal consequences when the time came to divide the inheritance (not that there would have been any after the 15 children) and at other times important to the law.

Thus, marriage has only two sources of civil legitimacy—the common law and legislation, which generally means state legislation. Religion does not enter into this discussion. If two gay people want to form a religion, or some current or future religion wants to recognize gay marriage, then government will have little, if any, interest in preventing them from having a religious ceremony to effectuate their union. The Massachusetts Supreme Court recognized that marriage is either what the common law or the legislature says it is:

> We begin by considering the nature of civil marriage itself. Simply put, the government creates civil marriage. In Massachusetts, civil marriage is, and since pre-Colonial days has been, precisely what its name implies: a wholly secular institution. See Commonwealth v. Munson, 127 Mass. 459, 460-466 (1879) (noting that "[i]n Massachusetts, from very early times, the requisites of a valid marriage have been regulated by statutes of the Colony, Province, and Commonwealth," and surveying marriage statutes from 1639 through 1834). No religious ceremony has ever been required to validate a Massachusetts marriage. Id.

> In a real sense, there are three partners to every civil marriage: two willing spouses and an approving State. See DeMatteo v. DeMatteo, 436 Mass. 18, 31 (2002) ("Marriage is not a mere contract between two parties but a legal status from which certain rights and obligations arise"); Smith v. Smith, 171 Mass. 404, 409 (1898) (on marriage, the parties "assume new

relations to each other and to the State"). See also French v. McAnarney, 290 Mass. 544, 546 (1935). While only the parties can mutually assent to marriage, the terms of the marriage—who may marry and what obligations, benefits, and liabilities attach to civil marriage—are set by the Commonwealth. Conversely, while only the parties can agree to end the marriage (absent the death of one of them or a marriage void ab initio), the Commonwealth defines the exit terms. See G.L. c. 208.

When Courts start numbering things, it is a warning sign that they are outside their area. At the risk of legal honesty, a court has no more business telling a legislature what sex married people can be than it does what number can be married. There is no intellectually honest conclusion to the contrary.

Liberals believe in vast personal freedom, and we refuse to be shackled to the past, as Conservatives are, when justice dictates. After all, like any other human invention, the laws serve humanity, not the other way around. However, society requires stability, and we Liberals must give due deference (though that hardly means all deference) to society's traditions and mores. Because the common law did not include same-sex marriage, and because marriage is a creature of the legislature, it is up to the legislature to change it.

This is the perfect situation in which to apply the "Liberal Federalism." If same-sex marriage is a good idea, where better to start it than in Vermont, which has something similar, or Massachusetts, the First Among Equals of Liberalism? If same-sex marriage cannot pass the Massachusetts Legislature, it has no legs. If it can pass, and the idea has merit, it will catch on with the other states. Marriage before the Massachusetts decision was a social experiment which, for all its problems, has been the subject of a considerable body of long-standing civil law. Same-sex marriage is now in the experimental stage. Only the future will tell if its results make sense. This is not an issue of personal freedom; it is a question of a change to an institution whose parameters are set only by legislatures. Although various legislatures could pass lots of different marriage laws that would violate the national or a particular state Constitution, that does not mean that we should automatically consider all changes Constitutional in nature, even if important. In fact, one of our fundamental legal principles is that we resort to a Constitutional analysis last, not first, so as not to trivialize the Constitution.

Whether or not the Massachusetts Legislature, or that of any other state, does institute same-sex marriage, do not expect Conservatives to accept it as the principled way of making the change. No, they will fall back upon their "not-mentioned-in-the-Constitution" argument and their moral arguments, and they'll urge that Massachusetts's same-sex marriages not receive the full faith and credit of the other States. They will then appeal to the United States Supreme Court, which by then may have a very conservative majority, to find a reason, under the United States Constitution, for those same-sex marriages not to be honored. Wait and see; that's what we can expect from the "strict constructionists."

To some extent, but with an important saving grace, Liberals followed the same mistaken path in the landmark abortion decision of *Roe v. Wade.* Conservatives are absolutely right that the decision was an illegal piece of legislation. We know it is legislation, because it has different rules for whether a woman can have an abortion in the first, second, or third trimester of her pregnancy. Again, courts' numbers are a warning signal of thin ice here. The case held that prior to the end of the first trimester the abortion decision must be left to the medical judgment of the woman's doctor, then until the end of the second trimester the state may reasonably regulate abortion related to the woman's health, and beginning with the third trimester the state may regulate and even proscribe abortion except where necessary to preserve the life or health of the mother. Law school 101 says that setting deadlines or temporally segmenting rights is a *legislative* function. There is nothing magic about a "trimester." If the Supreme Court had said that a woman could do "x" for 87 days, then "y" for 94 days, and finally "z" for 91 days, then the legislative nature of the decision would have been more obvious, but dividing things into "trimesters" doesn't make it less so. Here, again, basing the decision in part upon a dishonest approach to the law, and as a practical matter allowing the Supreme Court to pass legislation divided into segments of time, demeaned the decision and, to some extent, rightly lost legitimacy in the eyes of the public.

Conservatives, however, have an even more erroneous approach to *Roe v. Wade,* which is symptomatic of a broader conceptual problem in their legal analysis. First, it is obvious that most opposition to the abortion decision is based on the fact that abortion is morally repugnant to many people, which is a respectable position. However, Conservatives have taken the position that they can impose their moral position on everyone else, despite the Constitution's clear prohibition of doing just that.

Conservatives have reacted with horror that the Supreme Court based "a woman's right to choose" in the *Roe v. Wade* decision in substantial part upon the Ninth Amendment's simple language that "the enumeration in the Constitution, of certain rights, shall not be construed to deny or disparage others retained by the people." As Ann Coulter succinctly expressed it:

> The nation embarked on its abortion holocaust in 1973, when the Supreme
> Court astonished the nation by suddenly discovering that the Constitution
> mandated a right to abortion, despite there being nothing anyplace in the
> Constitution vaguely hinting at abortion.[12]

This is one of the most nonsensical "legal" concepts anyone ever attempted
to foist upon an unsuspecting public, and no real lawyer would ever say such a
thing except in a comedy routine. Airplanes and metal detectors are not in the
Constitution; traffic laws are not in the Constitution; draconian drug laws are
not in the Constitution. Why, not even Ann Coulter is mentioned by name in
the Constitution, not even once. And, yet, Ann Coulter has rights because she
fits in a group or groups that are mentioned—a person born here, a person
"naturally" born here, and a person within the jurisdiction, and so on. Our
Constitution is like *every* other legal document ever produced in the American
legal system, in that lawyers make analogies when adapting law to new or different situations.

Indeed, as a matter of simple logic, the fact that abortion is *not* mentioned
in the Constitution gives credence to the argument that it is a woman's inherent right under the Ninth Amendment (the enumeration in the Constitution
that certain rights shall not be construed to deny or disparage others retained
by the people). The weaker argument is that its absence means it is not a right.
Moreover, if we look at the question through the Coulter/Conservative lens,
we would have to substitute the Library of Congress (or now, perhaps the
Internet) for the Constitution in order to include every possible topic *not*
addressed. The Constitution is our nation's skeleton; it is not meant to be the
whole being in the flesh.

Coulter's Constitutional concepts also fail to grasp an important societal
value that you would think a Conservative, so interested in order, would
appreciate. That value is flexibility, mimicking nature's rule that a tree that
doesn't bend, breaks. The rigid Conservative mind cannot imagine that the
Constitution left many matters in the gray area of policy and society to be
determined in the give-and-take of electoral politics, in the courts, through
the use of executive power, or a combination of some or all of them, in no particular proportion. In fact, this is the only justification for the use of the Commerce Clause to uphold civil rights—society as a whole thought it was better
to get the job done somehow, rather than to wait for the South to catch up or

---

12. *Ibid.*

pressure such as civil turmoil to do the job. Expediency has its uses. It is a legitimate function of legal analysis to begin where Coulter begins, to see if the matter is directly addressed in the Constitution. But that is not the end of the inquiry, as any capable lawyer knows. There is a tension between the 9th Amendment and former laws that made abortion a crime. That does not preclude the Supreme Court from finding that abortion laws violated the Constitution, because declaring criminal laws unconstitutional is itself part of the Constitution. Respectable arguments can be made on both sides of that Constitutional issue, but Coulter's denigration of the 9th Amendment does a distinct disservice to the Constitution that she claims to "conserve."

In the Conservative viewpoint, as expressed by Coulter, "everyone knew the decision in *Roe v. Wade* was a joke. The decision hinged on the convenient notion of privacy, which, oddly enough, still fails to protect my right to manufacture methamphetamine, saw off shotgun barrels or euthanize the elderly, privately or otherwise."[13] Indeed, Coulter laments:

> In the past few years, federal courts have proclaimed a right to sodomy (not in the Constitution), a right to partial-birth abortion (not in the Constitution), a right not to have a Democratic governor recalled (not in the Constitution), a right not to gaze upon the Ten Commandments in an Alabama courthouse (not in the Constitution), a ban on the words "under God" in the Pledge of Allegiance (not in the Constitution), and a ban on voluntary student prayers at high school football games (not in the Constitution).[14]

But Coulter overlooks that methamphetamine, sawed-off shotguns, and euthanasia are not mentioned in the Constitution, either. Neither is sodomy, partial birth abortion, a right *not to* have a Democratic governor recalled (political parties are not mentioned in the Constitution), a right *to* gaze upon the Ten Commandments in an Alabama courthouse (Alabama is not in the Constitution), a direction to add the words "under G-d" in the Pledge of Allegiance (we got along fine when the Constitution was written without any pledge at all, much less one that mentions G-d), nor a direction to have voluntary student prayers at high school football games (football is not in the Constitution). It is strange how these strict constructionists are so flexible on issues

---

13. *Ibid.*
14. *Ibid.*

about which they care greatly. Both Liberals and Conservatives should just recognize the gray area that the Constitution wisely left for matters that are more or less subject to private conscience or legitimate differences of moral opinion.

The Liberal strategy regarding abortion is clear. There is a good or better chance that the candidate favored by the Conservatives will win the Presidency in 2004 and will appoint two or more members of the Supreme Court. Those members, openly or covertly, will have taken a pledge to the President to overturn *Roe v. Wade*. Therefore, Liberals should be versatile and put aside the Constitutional arguments, because they will fail, and *Roe v. Wade* will be overturned. Liberals will have to shift gears—and they should do so before those members are ever appointed—by beginning immediately to pass pro-abortion laws in the state legislatures. Some of these laws can be expected to be more restrictive than others—some much more restrictive. States may criminalize abortion entirely. But it's the legislative game or no game, and it's some laws or no laws.

Here again, though, do not expect Conservatives to conform to the standards they have laid down in attacking *Roe v. Wade*. Their attack has been that the matter is one for state legislatures, not the Supreme Court. Whereas from a legal view this argument has merit, if the Supreme Court overturns the abortion decision, the Conservatives will jettison their "legislation" argument. The Court will find, or Conservatives will begin a campaign to later have the Court find, that abortion not only is neither protected by nor mentioned in the Constitution, but is *contrary* to it. Thus, they will try to outlaw abortion through the same process they have objected to—the Court. Hypocrisy will rear its head, but it remains to be seen whether it will be successful. Perhaps with seven or eight votes on the Court, hypocrisy will prevail.

Conservatives certainly know how to use the courts to legislate when it comes to taking away the rights of ordinary people pitted against government and big companies. Juries are supposed to award damages on a case-by-case basis. Your automobile accident is not the same as anyone else's, so the damages should be different depending on the conclusions reached by the jury, even if it appears you and someone else have similar injuries. Otherwise, there is no purpose to a trial; if similar injuries automatically deserve similar awards, the matter can be taken out of the legal system entirely and given over to some administrative board. This is already what is done with most workplace injuries. Such an administrative board, and the standards for the awards, can be created only by statute, not judges—in theory. However, in vogue in many of the Circuit Courts, which generally hear federal cases from multiple states—and as the courts become more conservative, it may be all of them, plus the Supreme Court—is to engage in the wholesale "remitting" of cases. That means the Circuit Courts find that jury awards are too big and return the cases to the District Courts with orders to reduce the damages. The theory properly arose to redress injustice in particular cases, where the jury's passions were so inflamed that it awarded a dollar amount sure to drive a company out of business and take with it hundreds of jobs, while giving a windfall to the plaintiff. But now, Conservative courts are abusing the proper exercise of this power to make social policy. Especially in civil rights cases—which include all sorts of controversies, such as freedom of speech, not just racial discrimination—these courts command that if someone is fired in retaliation for speaking out against an improper government action, s/he will receive "x" dollars, because that is what the last person who spoke out and was fired received. Juries have been reduced to mere finders of whether defendants are liable. The question of how much in damages a plaintiff should be awarded has been usurped by Conservative judges, who were put on the bench to protect their fellow government employees, the rich, and the powerful.

Liberals did fail to show Conservatives the respect they are due on the abortion question, in that most Conservatives are motivated on the issue by what they believe is a matter of morals. In return, Conservatives have failed to give Liberals any respect for the Liberal position, which is also formed as a moral decision. Conservatives, and some or many Liberals, might believe that there is a moral duty to raise a child that was conceived through rape, born with a severe birth defect, born to suffocating poverty, or born to a parent who will very possibly beat it to death or otherwise abuse it. Liberals and some Conservatives might believe to the contrary. The Liberal resolution of the question, however, is either the more appropriate one, or at least due the same respect from Conservatives that their view on the issue deserves. The Liberals' resolution is to leave this difficult decision to the pregnant woman, not the government. And as abortion is not mentioned in the Constitution, even under the Conservatives' theory, the government should leave the decision to the woman.

What Coulter is really after is women's birth control pills and other means of preventing unwanted pregnancies and this goes for married people, not just the teenagers Coulter might claim to protect. Before *Roe v. Wade's* declaration of a right to privacy under the 9th Amendment, there was *Griswold v. Connecticut*, which declared that the government had no right to tell people whether they could use birth control. Birth control is not mentioned in the Constitution, either, and yet, almost no one thinks the local gendarme has the right to crash into your bedroom under some "probable cause" (such as your having a small number of children in proportion to the number of years you have been married) to determine whether you are using birth control. There is no theoretical difference in Constitutional analysis between this issue and the battle over abortion. So, if you believe that it is your choice whether to use birth control, you are not a Conservative. Don't be fooled that they are after anything less, whether you are married or single, male or female.

Liberals should not go down the same path as the Coulters of the more-reactionary-than-usual Conservatives by distorting a document that already reflects all of our values. Liberals' approach to gun control, however, does venture down that path.

Using a tactic similar to the "Commerce Clause" argument, Liberals have begun to attack guns under "tort" law—trying to run gun manufacturers out of business by holding them responsible for gun-inflicted damage under the theory that their products are "inherently dangerous." A "tort" is a civil, as opposed to a criminal, wrong; it says the injured party is another legal person, not society as a whole. The "inherently dangerous" theory normally applies to such things as lawn darts—those giant darts with huge metal points that stick in the ground when thrown at the Fourth of July barbeque. They're supposed to stick in the ground, but sometimes, they stick in Grandma. A lawn dart might be inherently dangerous, because when used for the purpose for which it was intended, a game, it can have an unintended consequence—a hole in Grandma filled by a large metal point. Because the consequence of the intended use is not intended, the manufacturer, not just the user, may have some civil liability for the damage caused. A gun is something different. It is meant to create a large hole in Grandpa when he makes a bad joke around Grandma, and so the manufacturer should not be held responsible when it performs as intended. The anti-gun lawsuits are therefore built upon a dishonest premise, which fosters disrespect for the law.

This does not mean that guns are not a problem, or that gun control is wrong. Conservatives, who continue to condemn children in gang-ridden neighborhoods to drive-by shootings by refusing to control guns, fail to meet their social responsibilities—as usual. However, Liberals need to meet this issue head-on and make the necessary reform without stooping to undermining our system in order to save it.

Gun proponents like to scream that gun control is unconstitutional. And they are right, in a way. A fair reading of the 2nd Amendment and its history is that the government—the *federal* government, that is—is barred from "infringing" on the right of "the People" to keep and bear arms. The gun lobbyists are also correct in asserting that this right is meant to keep the federal government at bay the next time Hitler takes over the White House. We cannot, for the sake of convenience, just gloss over what the Founders wanted where that intent (1) is clear, and (2) has not been modified by amendment, including the seismic Constitutional changes caused by the Civil War. We have to work within the Constitutional framework if we do not want to harm the integrity of our system by "end runs" around the law as surely as the guns harm it by killing and maiming our fellow citizens.

There is a simple solution to gun control that is Constitutional, yet will take away the right of every urban gang member, alienated suburban brat, and country weirdo to own a weapon—although with a gun for every man, woman, and child in the country already out there, even this solution won't end the problem entirely. For all those who spend their time imagining the final battle against a future evil White House, the solution is to give them the chance to be real soldiers, so that when the time comes for that fight, they can do us some good (and pick up highway litter and sandbag overflowing rivers in the meantime).

Working within the system and controlling guns is not hard to accomplish. The primary focus of the 2nd Amendment is that the serious business of overthrowing a dictator necessitates tight organization and, therefore, should be carried out by the states. Their success eliminates the need for "the People" to act as the bulwark against a dictatorial Washington. The right to keep and bear arms is rightly part of a system of "well-regulated" state militias. But our system provides for the 50 *elected* governors, leading state armies, to free us from the next Mr. Hitler, not the President of the National Rifle Association, leading a band of unorganized citizens. Only if a state's governor throws in his or her lot with the Washington dictator does the right to oppose by force of arms devolve to the People, and even then the Constitutional object is to align the well-regulated militia of one state with an elected governmental leader from another state.

State Legislatures could adopt the following Uniform Well-Regulated Militia Act. In sum, the provisions I have drafted say that if you want a gun, you have to serve in the National Guard for six weeks every year at the rate of $75 per week, or whatever other sum a state can afford. While on duty, but not at war, this well-regulated militia can clean up the slums, build dams, dig ditches, spruce up railway tracks, help the elderly and disabled to get to the hospital or get food, and perform myriad other socially useful tasks.

This law will require anyone desiring to own a gun to take courses on its care and its responsible use. All those wishing to own a gun by joining the militia (called the National Guard in most places) will also have to study the federal and state Constitutions and criminal law regarding guns, so that when they go on the march against Mr. Hitler, they will know why they are going and exactly what it is they are protecting—a liberal, tolerant, democratic, capitalistic society that rejects racism and is operated for the general welfare of all the people. If someone commits a crime with a National Guard gun, the militia member appointed to the gun will be charged with failing to secure property important to the preservation of our liberty and appropriately punished if convicted.

Under this proposed law, the governor of each state, as Commander-in-Chief of the militia, can determine when and where each member may use his or her gun and where to store it. Thus, you may never get to see your weapon, at least until the Governor decides that the best strategy to re-take Washington is to have you charge the Washington Monument with guns blazing.

Most important, if anyone possesses a gun other than through this well-regulated militia plan, the idea is to slap him or her in the hoosgow, and for a long time. This will work, if anyone has the guts to clean up Dodge City America. The following is the proposed text of the Uniform Well-Regulated Militia Act.

Preamble

The Legislature recognizes that the proliferation of arms among its citizenry has endangered life and limb among those citizens, as well as other residents of, and visitors to, this State. The Legislature does recognize that the Second Amendment to the Constitution of the United States bars the United States from infringing upon the right of the People of the United States to keep and bear arms. However, the Legislature also recognizes that this prohibition of the United States Constitution does not apply to the State of the Union; rather, the States have the right to control the right to keep and bear arms through a "well-regulated militia." The Legislature has therefore determined to attempt to keep life and limb in this State safer by regulating the rights of persons to keep and bear arms in this State through its militia, the National

Guard. It is the intention of the Legislature that no person in this State shall keep or bear arms other than in compliance with this Act.

Sec. 1A. No person who is neither a citizen of this State nor has declared his or her intention to become a citizen of this State may keep or bear arms in this State. Any such person who is, or intends to be, a citizen of this State shall be known under this Act as a "Qualified-Potential Arms Owner." Only a natural person may be a Qualified-Potential Arms Owner.

Sec. 1B. No Qualified-Potential Keeper and Bearer of Arms may actually own or possess arms in this State except as provided in this Act. Any Qualified-Potential Arms Owner who actually owns or possesses arms in this State shall be known under this Act as an "Arms Owner."

Sec. 1C. No Arms Owner may own any type of arms other than those prescribed by the Commander-in-Chief and the Adjutant General of this State in the customary chain of command. It is the intent of the Legislature that such arms be as uniform as possible in keeping with the proper defense of this State and the United States.

Sec. 1D. The Commander-in-Chief and the Adjutant General, through orders given in the customary chain of command, shall implement a system whereby the State is aware at all times of each individual arm issued to and possessed by Arms Owners. Without limitation, each Arms Owner shall at all times be responsible for keeping the National Guard informed of the location and condition of the arms issued to him or her. The Commander-in-Chief and the Adjutant General may order, from time to time and/or at all times, that any and/or all arms in this State be stored at a specific location or locations. Beginning 1 year after the date hereof, and concluding as quickly as possible thereafter, all arms not authorized hereby to be in the possession of an Arms Owner shall be condemned at market value and taken into the possession of the National Guard under orders prescribed by the Commander-in-Chief and the Adjutant General in the customary chain of command.

Sec. 2A. During the time they are Arms Owners in this State, all such persons are permanent Members of the National Guard.

Sec. 2B. During the time they are Members of the National Guard, each Arms Owner shall serve six weeks in active duty in each calendar year. The dates of such active duty for each Arms Owner shall be established by the Commander-in-Chief and the Adjutant General through the customary chain of command. Each Arms Owner also shall be subject to call to active duty the same as any other member of the National Guard. Any Arms Owner who avoids or schemes to avoid his or her duty to serve six weeks of active duty in each calendar year or any other call to active duty by moving from state to state, or otherwise, shall be subject to serving two years of continuous active service and/or forfeiture of his or her right to keep and/or bear arms for the remainder of his or her natural life, or both, and/or fine, confinement, or punishment under the military laws of this State the same as any other military personnel who is absent without leave.

Sec. 2C. During the annual six weeks' active duty in each calendar year, and in addition to any other military training and/or duties prescribed by the Commander-in-Chief and the Adjutant General in the customary chain of command, each Arms Owner shall receive training in marksmanship, arms maintenance, the federal and state Constitutions, citizenship, responsible use of arms, and state and federal criminal law relating to arms.

Sec. 2D. During such time as they are on active duty, each Arms Owner shall receive compensation at the rate of $75 per week.

Sec. 3A. Each Arms Owner is responsible to keep his or her arms from any person (a) who is not authorized to keep and/or bear them and (b) who is not authorized by the National Guard to possess the particular arm in question. If any civilian or military crime is committed with the arm issued to an Arms Owner by a person or persons other than the Arms Owner, then upon conviction by a general court martial, and in addition to any other sentence for the underlying crime or crimes committed with the arm, the responsible Arms Owner may be sentenced to up to 10 years in the county jail, and if committed by the Arms owner, up to 25 years.

*   *   *

This solution ought to satisfy everybody. The NRA can have its guns, the States' Righters can have their States' Rights, the Liberals can have their socially active domestic training program, and everyone can have safer streets. Moreover, when Hitler takes over Washington, maybe we can even beat him.

Our strength as a country lies in this sort of flexible adherence to the Constitution, including its amendments. There is no doubt that the formation of this country, including the ideals of the Declaration of Independence and the genius of the Constitution, was the single greatest secular step in the establishment of human dignity in the earth's history. Any flaws simply reflect the Founders' upbringing. Conservatives believe that childhood environment and personal problems never excuse bad adult behavior or justify extending mercy (except for drug-abusing-right-wing radio personalities, perhaps), but we Liberals should grant this mercy even for Conservatives (except for *hypocritical* drug-abusing-right-wing radio personalities).

In context, the acts of those white men in Philadelphia and elsewhere as the nation was being formed earned the world's gratitude forever. Yes, they failed to end slavery for black people and even entrenched it, and they restricted voting to white males who owned real property. Yet, only a blink of an eye earlier in historical terms, virtually every white man and woman was also a slave wearing, quite literally, the iron collar of serfdom. The King ruled absolute. Later, the nobles gained some power with the Magna Carta. The sculpture of freedom began to emerge as entrenched power was chipped away, little by little, until our revolution when, tired of the slow progress, the settlers threw away the chisel and sand-blasted their way to faster progress (obviously powered by some special bellows fashioned by Ben Franklin—a Liberal's Liberal, by the way). But, the job's not finished yet.

Conservatives, always trying to retain power in the entrenched few, are pushing their judicial agenda on the rest of us by forming a club known as "The Federalist Society." To Conservatives, the name evokes memories of a supposedly golden age, a time when an exclusive group of white men in wigs and satin pants could get together and debate which rights they, the federal government, and the states should have, as opposed to everyone else, who would receive the rights granted to them by the wise white men, including the right to remain a slave. This is a Conservative's ideal social order. By joining this club, a member is properly branded for future use in the war against a Liberal society, sort of like a Good Housekeeping seal of approval for having a sufficiently rigid world outlook.

These are among the Federalist Society's "principles" as delineated on its website:

- That it is emphatically the province and duty of the judiciary to say what the law is, not what it should be;

- That the constitutional scheme did not contemplate the imposition by fiat of the legislative preferences of members of the judiciary, under the banner of "societal evolution";

- That this type of judicial legislating, being insulated from the check of popular support, has been a key instrument in the expansion of federal governmental power;

- That this expansion has been at the expense of individuals' abilities to control their own destinies, and of intermediate institutions such as families, churches, personal property, and the states, which helped to shield people from the government's full force;...[15]

This is the same old crooning for States' Rights, which means local ability to oppress and discriminate against those who oppose elite rich people. It's the same old Conservatives' game. You can dress up States' Rights, but Liberals must see to it that it never makes it to the prom, because it still belongs in detention. Oh, one last "Federalist" principle:

> And that the true purpose of the legal order is to ensure that the power conferred upon the state is used to secure people's lives and goods, the true purpose of an independent judiciary is to prevent the rigging of the legal order into an extension of the sovereign's will, and that neither the legal order nor the judiciary is presently serving these purposes....[16]

That principle is more inane than States' Rights. The word "rigging" aside, if the purpose of law is not to extend the sovereign's will, then it has no purpose. We can legitimately argue night and day about the extent and wisdom of the sovereign's will—but when you get arrested, the sovereign sure is extending its will upon you, and when you seek to enforce a private contract, you're asking for the sovereign to extend its will to help you. Instead of the sovereign's police officers making arrests, we could ask Afghan warlords to do it for us, or in the case of private contract enforcement, we could have the right to forego court cases and simply have the right to throttle our debtors until they pay us. That particular "principle" also states, "Neither the legal order nor the judiciary is presently serving these purposes" (securing our lives and goods). Now, all or nearly all of these Federalists, being drawn from law schools and the legal profession, are most likely making their living in the legal system, so there must be plenty of law going on to protect their goods. As far as protecting lives, the life of the average non-Federalist Society lawyer is a lot more at risk than the life of the average Federalist Society lawyer. At least no "Death

---

15. "Federalist Principles" (Washington: The Federalist Society for Law & Public Policy Studies, 1994), *Chicago-Kent College of Law Online*, at http://www.kentlaw.edu/student_orgs/fedsoc/Principles.htm
16. *Ibid.*

Row Project" information appeared on the Federalist Society's website, although there were links to these websites, among others:

The Heritage Foundation
Conservative Political Action Conference (CPAC)
The Family Research Council
Conservative News Service (CNS)
FOX News Channel
George Will Articles
National Review
Media Research Center[17]

If those people and companies don't have their property properly protected by "the sovereign" right now, it is only because they own almost all of it, so there isn't enough sovereign to do the job for them, and they can afford to buy their own private protection. They should get to doing that right away, because paying for all their own services, and eschewing all the benefits of the sovereign, will build their individual characters.

Who are the most prominent members of the Federalist Society? Among others are: Robert Bork, the unsuccessful Supreme Court nominee, who during the Watergate scandal instead of asking for Nixon's resignation, fired the independent counsel investigating the matter; Linda Chávez, an ardent opponent of affirmative action; Judge Posner and his philosophical twin on the Court of Appeals for the Seventh Circuit, Frank Easterbrook; Senator Orrin Hatch, ranking Republican on the Senate Judiciary Committee who pushes forward all the Conservative Court nominees; Don Hodel, a past president of the Christian Coalition; Charles Murray, author of *The Bell Curve*, a 1994 book that claims some races are less intelligent than others; Antonin Scalia, Supreme Court Justice (who goes fishing with Dick Cheney even while Cheney has a case pending before him); David Sentelle, a protoge of Sen. Jesse Helms; and Kenneth Starr, special prosecutor.[18] A more complete roster is set forth on Appendix A.

---

17. *Ibid.*
18. "The Federalist Society: From Obscurity to Power," *People For the American Way*, at http://www.pfaw.org/pfaw/general/ default.aspx?oid=780

Liberals should not be complacent about the Federalist Society, because it has not only important government power behind it, but also big dollars at its disposal. As co-authors George Curry and Trevor Coleman observe, the Federalist Society stretches deep into corporate America, as well as the judiciary, claiming as members of its business advisory counsel such persons as the president of Media General Cable, the board chair of giant Wachovia Corp., the CEO of Geneva Steel, major players at Morgan Stanley financial services, Bank of America, Sony Corporation, General Motors, GTE, Metropolitan Life, Exxon (of Valdez fame), and the National Football League's counsel for litigation.[19]

Federalist Society member "Richard Posner, Judge on the U.S. Court of Appeals for the Seventh Circuit and a senior lecturer at the University of Chicago Law School," represents well the Conservatives' truly radical judicial philosophy. Posner in a moment of candor, served up in a cookbook the legal principles that he and, presumably, his movement, hold dear:

> Fifth, law is an activity rather than a concept or a group of concepts. No bounds can be fixed a priori on what shall be allowed to count as an argument in law. The modern significance of natural law is not as a body of objective norms that underwrite positive law but as a source of the ethical and political arguments that judges use to challenge, change, or elaborate positive law—in other words to produce new positive law. There are no moral "reals" (at least none available to decide difficult legal cases), but neither is there a body of positive law that somehow preexists the judicial decisions applying, and in the process of confirming, modifying, extending, and rejecting, the "sovereign's" commands. The line between positive law and natural law is no longer interesting or important and the concepts themselves are jejune…. Sixth…There are no "logically" correct interpretations; interpretation is not a logical process…. Seventh, there are no overarching concepts of justice that our legal system can seize upon to give direction to the enterprise….[20]

Posner says that the law is whatever the Conservatives say it is. Their entire fire-breathing about "strict construction" is a farce and a fraud, because unlike Liberals, who truly believe in a strict construction of our Liberal Constitution,

---

19. Curry and Emerge at http://www.ratical.org/ratville/CAH/ hijakjustice.html

20. Richard A. Posner, *The Problems of Jurisprudence* (Harvard University Press, 1990), 459-460.

the so-called Conservatives want to read into that document, forever re-forged in the battles of the Civil War, a narrow outlook that justifies the continued rule by rich oligarchies in their little despotic local governments, and precedent be damned.

And whom does Judge Posner hold up as one of his heroes? None other than Ann Coulter, named by Posner as one of the top 100 Public Intellectuals of 2001.[21] What a pair.

In one article Coulter argues that the President of the United States should simply disregard Supreme Court rulings when s/he disagrees with them. This is reminiscent of Nixon's statement prior to the Supreme Court's ruling on whether he could keep secret the damning Watergate Tapes, when Nixon said that he had to follow only a "definitive" Supreme Court ruling. Conservatives hailed that statement even though Nixon averted a battle over it by turning over the tapes. Coulter argues that *Roe v. Wade* is one such decision a President could disregard. She writes: "Even when dealing with lawless tyrants [she means the Supreme Court Justices, most of whom have been appointed by Conservative Presidents, as Coulter herself points out!], conservatives have a fetish about following the law."[22] If Conservatism stands for anything decent, it is in establishing good order. Thus, Coulter and her other Federalist Society cohorts are tearing down that bulwark of our Republic as well, by advocating the position that following the law as declared by our courts is a mere voluntary act.

The combination of Posner's Conservative legal philosophy, which denies the possibility of "moral reals" or "overarching concepts of justice that our legal system can seize upon to give direction to the enterprise," with Coulter's nonsense of justice is destroying our legal system. The Conservatives' radical agenda for all federal courts is testing its wings everywhere, but its most extreme incubator is the United States Court of Appeals for the Fourth Circuit, centered in Richmond, Virginia, not very coincidentally the capital of Jefferson Davis's Confederacy. "And as recently as 1999, Chief Justice William H. Rehnquist led the Fourth Circuit's annual judicial conference in a traditional rousing singalong that included 'Dixie,'" Deborah Sontag writes.[23]

---

21. http://www.anncoulter.org/bio.html
22. Coulter, "Supreme Court Opinions Not Private Enough," at http://www.humaneventsonline.com/article.php?id=2533
23. Deborah Sontag, "The Power of the Fourth," *New York Times Magazine*, March 9, 2003, 40.

The "Thurmond" problem raises its ugly head here, too. George W. Bush's most recent nomination for that Court, who now sits there, is Dennis W. Shedd, a former Thurmond Chief of Staff.[24] Judge Karen Williams, another Judge in that Circuit, Sontag reports, was nominated by the first President Bush upon Thurmond's recommendation, and when she was sworn in, "Thurmond and her father-in-law reminisced about how they used to double-date."[25] The Fourth Circuit was not racially integrated on the bench until 2001, although it has the largest African-American population of any federal appellate jurisdiction.[26] Judge Williams said that Thurmond wanted her to be the first woman on the Fourth Circuit Bench, because he "liked to be on the cutting edge, and he just plain liked women too."[27] Thurmond did like women, but he thought some, like his own daughter, should not use the same drinking fountain as others. Judge William W. Wilkins, Jr., was a Thurmond aide and campaign director.

Race played a large role in the Fourth Circuit's makeup during the Clinton years. Clinton's four white nominees were approved by the Senate.[28] However, every one of Clinton's four African-American nominees to the Court was blocked by a group of Senators, usually led by arch-Conservative Senator Jesse Helms.[29] Both Helms and Thurmond denied that the blocking of these nominees had anything to do with race.[30] Neither, we would then have to assume, did Thurmond's failure publicly to acknowledge his daughter during his lifetime.

It would be a mistake to say that the fourth Circuit's judges, as Conservatives in general, "just don't get it," because the Fourth Circuit does get it; it just doesn't like it, and takes Lee's surrender at Appomattox Courthouse as a mere lull in the hostilities. Among other things, the Fourth Circuit has ruled that the Virginia Military Institute (Stonewall Jackson's old stomping grounds, naturally enough) may remain an all male institution, as long as women are given separate but comparable education (sound familiar?), and

---

24. *Ibid.*, 40.
25. *Ibid.*, 41.
26. *Ibid.*, 41.
27. *Ibid.*, 41.
28. *Ibid.*, 45.
29. *Ibid.*, 45.
30. *Ibid.*, 45.

overturned a Virginia prohibition against license plates bearing the Confederate flag.[31]

The basis for these types of decisions is the same troubling States' Rights
philosophy that has caused our country so much trouble—from Jefferson, to
Calhoun, Toombs, the Civil War, Jim Crow, and all the other ills it has
wrought. Sontag continues:

> "I don't go on the bench as liberal or conservative," [Fourth Circuit Judge J.
> Harvie] Wilkinson said. And yet he does not dispute that he is a conserva-
> tive jurist. He acknowledges his place among those who came of age con-
> cerned about "the excessive activism" of the Warren Court.... Yet with
> conservatives now controlling most of the nation's federal appeals courts,
> Wilkinson is one among many who have come to a new appreciation of
> judicial activism. Like the "new federalists" whose conservative thinking
> increasingly influences the legal mainstream, Wilkinson said he believes
> that the Constitution is more than just the Bill of Rights. He doesn't think
> that the Bill of Rights has been overemphasized, he is quick to say, but that
> what he calls "the structural Constitution" has been underemphasized.
> "That body of the document that spells out the relationship between the
> federal government and the states was neglected for far too long," he said.
> The power of Congress was seen as unlimited and that of the states as a vir-
> tual nullity." Wilkenson has found it exciting he said, to be engaged in
> redressing this imbalance, which sometimes means striking down Congres-
> sional acts that seem to usurp state power unconstitutionally.[32]

If America follows the lead of Conservatives in general, and the Fourth
Circuit in particular, we will find ourselves once again riven by Sectionalism—only this time those the local despots seek to oppress are going to be
"mad as hell, and they aren't going to take it any longer." The Conservatives
may then indeed get their wish, because if the federal government doesn't protect the average citizen from the power-hungry avarice of the state and local
tin pot dictators, the citizens will protect themselves. Liberalism is the lubrica-
tion that keeps the moving parts of this great country from rubbing against
each other with great friction, eventually burning up and then melting. If we
use Liberalism liberally, this great country will continue as such.

In contrast to the Conservatives' "do nothing so that we can continue to
exploit the weak" practices, which have only taken this country down the path

31. *Ibid.*, 42.
32. *Ibid.*, 65.

of civil war, beatings and lynchings, the Liberal philosophy of government has always strived to make the country a better place to live, and its reforms have succeeded in changing America for the better for everyone, including Conservatives.

Reason 3. Liberals Support the Active Federal Government Lincoln won for The People.

"Fascism was really the basis for the New Deal."—Ronald Reagan to *Time* Magazine, May 17, 1976

Conservatives Want To Rescind Our Social Contract

Our form of government is heavily influenced by the "social contract" theories of Jean Jacques Rousseau, Thomas Hobbes, and John Locke, with more emphasis on the last, the French gentleman being a little far out for most Americans' taste. The Internet Encyclopedia of Philosophy provides a concise definition of social contract theory:

> The definitive statement of social contract theory is found in Chapters 13 through 15 of Hobbes's Leviathan. Briefly, Hobbes argues that the original state of nature is a condition of constant war, which rational and self-motivated people would want to end. These people, then, will establish fundamental moral laws to preserve peace. The foundation of Hobbes's theory is the view that humans are psychologically motivated by only selfish interests. Hobbes argued that, for purely selfish reasons, the agent is better off living in a world with moral rules than one without moral rules. Without moral rules, we are subject to the whims of other people's selfish interests. Our property, our families, and even our lives are at continual risk. Selfishness alone will therefore motivate each agent to adopt a basic set of rules which will allow for a civilized community.[1]

As we saw earlier, the Civil War was fought over two types of "freedom," both claiming the "Spirit of '76" as the social contract upon which their societies were based. In the words of the Civil War soldiers quoted earlier, one side fought for freedom for all mankind; the other fought for the right of one race to enslave another, while claiming democratic rights for those with the right color skin and the right to be "free" from those who would take away their right to enslave. Fortunately, the Southerners' view of the social contract was rescinded on the battlefield, even though Conservatism still serves its unsavory provisions. The end result of the Civil War was to change the social contract then in existence—the original Constitution (including the first Ten Amendments)—to make the federal government the protector of last resort for our citizens' civil rights.

Unfortunately, this country's original social contract had other defects not cured on the battlefields of the Civil War. While it did not take another civil war to remove those provisions, it did take another upheaval, the Great Depression of the 1930s. This time, it was a Democratic President, Franklin Delano Roosevelt, who followed Lincoln's lead and once again rearranged the social contract to make the federal government the protector of last resort for the poor, the elderly, and the working people of the country. The social contract generated by the Great Depression provided that if American citizens remained loyal to capitalism—itself a system of competition—in its own time of crisis, capitalism would return their loyalty and provide minimum protections for individual citizens in their times of crisis when they could not compete. This meant enacting certain laws that would protect the population from bad business. Ironically, however, the changes Roosevelt included in the social contract made the country safe for *good* business as well.

As we shall see, however, even after all these years, Conservatives have not accepted these reforms and continue their unremitting fight to undo them—even the ones from which they have themselves so heavily benefitted. Just as we Liberals must protect Lincoln's changes in the American social contract, so must we protect those of Lincoln's heir, Roosevelt.

---

1.   "Social Contract," *Internet Encyclopedia of Philosophy*, ed. James Fieser and Bradley Dowden, at http://www.iep.utm.edu/s/soc-cont.htm

Protections For The Poor

Maybe you have read *Oliver Twist* by Charles Dickens, or perhaps at least have some image of it garnered from the play, *Oliver*. Though set in England, it demonstrates the concept of "welfare" before Franklin Roosevelt came along. "All we ever get is gruel, gru-el…" People were lucky to eat. No adequate social "safety nets" existed; it was the Poor House or nothing. In times of crisis, those in need depended on local handouts or local governments for survival. As the Constitutional Rights Foundation's website notes:

> Many believed that those who couldn't take care of themselves were to blame for their own misfortunes. During the 19th century, local and state governments as well as charities established institutions such as poorhouses and orphanages for destitute individuals and families. Conditions in these institutions were often deliberately harsh so that only the truly desperate would apply.

> Local governments (usually counties) also provided relief in the form of food, fuel, and sometimes cash to poor residents. Those capable were required to work for the town or county, often at hard labor such as chopping wood and maintaining roads. But most on general relief were poor dependent persons not capable of working: widows, children, the elderly, and the disabled.

> Local officials decided who went to the poorhouse or orphanage and who would receive relief at home. Cash relief to the poor depended on local property taxes, which were limited. Also, not only did a general prejudice exist against the poor on relief, but local officials commonly discriminated against individuals applying for aid because of their race, nationality, or religion. Single mothers often found themselves in an impossible situation. If they applied for relief, they were frequently branded as morally unfit by the community. If they worked, they were criticized for neglecting their children.

> In 1909, President Theodore Roosevelt called a White House conference on how to best deal with the problem of poor single mothers and their children. The conference declared that preserving the family in the home was preferable to placing the poor in institutions, which were widely criticized as costly failures.

> Starting with Illinois in 1911, the "mother's pension" movement sought to provide state aid for poor fatherless children who would remain in their own homes cared for by their mothers. In effect, poor single mothers would be excused from working outside the home. Welfare reformers argued that

the state pensions would also prevent juvenile delinquency since mothers would be able to supervise their children full-time.

By 1933, mother's pension programs were operating in all but two states. They varied greatly from state to state and even from county to county within a state. In 1934, the average state grant per child was $11 a month. Administered in most cases by state juvenile courts, mother's pensions mainly benefitted families headed by white widows. These programs excluded large numbers of divorced, deserted, and minority mothers and their children.

Few private and government retirement pensions existed in the United States before the Great Depression. The prevailing view was that individuals should save for their old age or be supported by their children. About 30 states provided some welfare aid to poor elderly persons without any source of income. Local officials generally decided who deserved old-age assistance in their community.[2]

This system wasn't very pretty. White people had created the Horatio Alger myth that anyone who wanted to work could and would find work and get rich. Black people—well, they didn't count, so they got Sambo for a myth.

In 1929, however, this myth came into conflict with the reality of world depression. A huge number of white people found out what it was like to be black in that even if they wanted to work, there wasn't any work to get—and it wasn't their fault, as everyone except rich white Conservatives recognized. As William E. Leutenberg describes it, Titans of Industry such as Henry Ford disclaimed any responsibility for their workers. Other Detroit businessmen concluded that if there was not enough money to support local relief, each recipient should just get less, and Titans such as John Edgerton, the President of the National Association of Manufacturers, blamed the workers for their plight.[3] The the only difference between Conservatives then and now is that

2. Constitutional Rights Foundation Bill of Rights in Action Summer 1998 (14:3), http://www.crf-usa.org/bria/bria14_3.html. The issue was made possible by a grant from the W.M. Keck Foundation. According to its own website, http://www.fdncenter.org, the W. M. Keck Foundation was established in 1954 by the late William Myron Keck, founder of the Superior Oil Company to support exemplary scientific, engineering, and medical research programs at accredited universities and colleges throughout the United States.

the current ones want to force people to gamble away their Social Security in the stock market, and then still blame them when it is lost.

In any event, more than 25% of the workforce had no job.[4] Thus, white people also found out, many for the first time, that when there is no money in the pocket, there is no food in the pantry. As also noted by the Constitutional Rights Foundation, about 18 million disadvantaged people lived at a bare subsistence level in the Unites States at the start of the Great Depression; a few years later that number had swelled by another 13 million. There were food riots and vastly increased homelessness. Children were affected the worst, with 20 percent of U.S. school children showing effects of poor nutrition, inadequate housing, and substandard medical care. Many schools closed for lack of funds, and 200,000 boys became beggars.[5]

In the 1960s, there was a joke that defined a Conservative as a Liberal who had been mugged. In the 1930s, the joke could have been that a Liberal was a Conservative who had lost his or her job.

The world's economy was in ruins, America was broke and surprisingly enough, America no longer loved everything about "limited government" or "local control." Americans came to equate those concepts with no hope, no progress and, in many cases, no shelter and no food. Leuchtenberg relates how 50 hungry men fought over garbage in the back of a Chicago restaurant, how some California men searched a city dump for half-rotted vegetables, and how scores of people in Salt Lake City were slowly starving, and their children kept out of school for lack of anything to wear.[6]

In fact, according to Leuchtenberg, "81 per cent of the children in white rural schools in Alabama were schooless; Georgia closed more than a thousand schools with an enrollment of over 170,000 pupils; Dayton schools in early 1933 opened only three days a week."[7]

---

3.   William E. Leuchtenberg, *Franklin D. Roosevelt and the New Deal* (New York, Evanston and London: Harper Torchbooks, The University Library, 1963), 21.

4.   Arthur M. Schlesinger, Jr., *The Coming of the New Deal* (Boston: Houghton Mifflin, 1957), 263.

5.   Constitutional Rights Foundation Bill of Rights in Action Summer 1998 (14:3), http://www.crf-usa.org/bria/bria14_3.html

6.   Leuchtenberg, 3.

7.   *Ibid.*, 21.

Most important, the Conservative myth that private charities and state and local government could handle problems unraveled, just as during the Civil War the earlier Conservative myth that state and local governments were the best protectors of freedom had. Historian Arthur Schlesinger describes how the existing relief system no longer worked, leading to the passage of the Emergency Relief and Construction Act in 1932. In some states, 40 percent of the people required this relief.[8]

Imagine more than 25% unemployment today, when a 6.5% rate earns harsh criticism of the Bush administration. Yet, the Conservative reaction was typically negative toward using Lincoln's federal government for any useful purpose. When Roosevelt first proposed $500 million in grants to states, rather than the aforementioned $300 million in loans, Schlesinger writes that it produced "violent reactions" such as those of John B. Hollister of Ohio, who plaintively asked whether anything was left "of our federal system," while Robert Luce of Massachusetts wondered, "Whether it is communism or not I do not know."[9]

When in doubt, Conservatives can be counted on to fall back on racism, and this time was no exception. Schlesinger adds: "There was considerable resentment, too, in farm areas, especially in the South. Planters complained that relief made it impossible to get cheap Negro farm labor."[10] The Conservatives also fell back on their usual cry for "local control," when the National Association of Manufacturers demanded that states run relief.[11]

Protections For The Elderly

Conservatives have *never* been *for* a program to assist elderly people unable to care for themselves. Their opposition to the very idea of Social Security has been unremitting, save for more recent lip-service necessitated by a desire for political survival. Schlesinger reports that at the beginning major business organizations such as the National Industrial Conference Board denounced the idea as socialistic; a General Motors representative called it an idea whose "dangers are manifest," and there were warnings by others of the final destruction of capitalism, with attendant moral decay, national bankruptcy, and the

---

8.   Schlesinger, 263
9.   *Ibid.*, 264.
10. *Ibid.*, 274.
11. *Ibid.*, 276.

end of the United States. According to Conservatives, Social Security meant the lash and slavery.[12] This was odd, because when they'd had their chance to oppose slavery, Conservatives had chosen to support it, even to the extent of *actually* trying to bring an end to the republic.

Conservative opposition to Social Security was built on the same foundation as Conservatism's opposition to every other progressive idea ever developed in this country: the desire of the few to keep as much of everything for themselves as possible—otherwise known as greed. Greed built and sustained slavery, and if Conservatives had anything to do with it, Washington would be held in its place, unable to help old people, as it would have been held unable to eliminate slavery or Jim Crow.

We all know now that the "manifest dangers" of Social Security did *not* come to pass. Far from undermining our national life by destroying initiative, thrift, and individual responsibility, Social Security strengthened the social contract, fostered more loyalty in citizens, and increased patriotism by keeping everyone on the team, even after their active days were completed. And, by *sharing*, rich people did not become poorer. They became far richer, as all now had a stake in the enterprise. Capitalism was hardly abandoned; rather, it defeated the other "isms," and has made most of its former enemies capitalist, to boot. We can argue whether there is more "moral decay" today; I think not, given that in the "golden age" one human could own another, but if there has been any decay, it is not attributable to allowing old people to eat. As far as feeling the lash of the dictator, that canard has also been proved false, but millions have been saved from the lash of hunger and living on the street—and no one [barely] subsisting on Social Security has yet taken over a Rockefeller or Gates mansion on those proceeds alone.

The Conservative position on Social Security was sad enough when it was newer—but at least Conservatives can plead ignorance in hindsight. What brings Liberals to tears today is that Conservatives have never given up the fight to bring down Social Security. All that has changed is the sales pitch, but the goal to destroy Social Security remains the same. Once Social Security had been in place for many years, Conservatives came to the conclusion that they could not defeat it head-on and therefore changed tactics to defeat it incrementally. William F. Buckley, Jr., again became the Conservatives' "intellectual" fount. Buckley's long-term attack was based upon a sailing analogy:

---

12. Ibid., 311-312.

A navigator for which two lighthouses can mark extreme points of danger relative to his present position, knows that by going back and making a wholly different approach, the two lighthouses will fuse together to form a single object to the vision, confirming the safety of his position. They are then said to be "in range." There is a point from which opposition to the social security laws and a devout belief in social stability are in range: as also a determined resistance to the spread of World Communism—and belief in political non-interventionism…a respect for the omnicompetence of the free market place—and the knowledge of the necessity for occasional inter-position.[13]

The analogy to sailing, a rich person's sport, was telling in and of itself. Then there also was the game-plan, still in effect and stated early, although stated in Buckley's usual arcane English: don't attack social security directly, because "social stability," i.e. the electorate, won't stand for it. Instead, Conservatives try to chip away at it until it can finally be brought down entirely.

One of the first chips was tapped out in the 1964 Presidential campaign, when the Republican candidate, Senator Barry M. Goldwater of Arizona, suggested making Social Security "voluntary":

"I would like to suggest one change, that Social Security be made voluntary, that if a person can provide better for himself, let him do it." This was the statement chiefly used against him in the campaign. It was, however, no spur-of-the-moment rejoinder to a question. No less than seven times Goldwater was on record, in some form or another—in interviews, articles, and the *Congressional Record*—with one or another variation of this idea, which he never repudiated.[14]

Like the Conservatives' fantasy that union membership can be voluntary within companies where a majority of the workers have voted to unionize, Social Security could not work if "voluntary." The very idea strikes at the heart of the social contract formulated in the Depression. When Ronald Reagan challenged Gerald Ford for the Republican nomination for President in 1976 because Ford was not conservative enough (imagine that!), Reagan followed in

---

13. John B. Judis, *William F. Buckley, Jr., Patron Saint of the Conservatives* (New York: Simon and Schuster, 1988), 168-169.

14. Theodore H. White, *The Making of the President 1964* (New York: Atheneum Publishers, 1965), 303.

the footsteps of Goldwater, his mentor, writes Reagan biographer, Steven Hayward:

> One of Reagan's ideas for reforming Social Security was to have some of its funds invested in the stock market, in the industrial might of nation's economy.[15]

On January 20, 2004, President Bush's State of the Union Address advocated allowing a portion of a person's Social Security contributions to be "invested" in the stock market, because historically the average return from the market has been higher than is received from regular social security benefits. "Average" is the key. Some people have their savings wiped out in the stock market, while others thrive, and still others tread water. Social Security is *not* an "investment" in the ordinary sense. Rather, it is the government's *guarantee* of a minimum return. The strength of Social Security is its lack of risk in exchange for a lower return. Making any part of Social Security a traditional investment undercuts its very nature. If Conservatives' idea to allow the investment in the stock market of some of a person's Social Security benefits is a good one, the logic for allowing all of it to be invested would be irrefutable.

Conservatives must be stopped before they slice off this piece of Social Security, or there will be none left sooner than you might think. "Voluntary" here, "private investment" there, the idea is always the same—to remove the federal government as the last guarantor of the elderly person's well-being and to make the elderly's place on our American team a thing of chance rather than certainty. Just as white Southerners ought to bend down and thank African-Americans for forcing them under penalty of law to become rich beyond their wildest dreams by breaking the back of segregation, so ought Conservatives and capitalists thank Liberals for smoothing out the wrinkles and inequities in the capitalist system, through such programs as Social Security, to make this country safe for big business.

And, yet, the Conservative battering ram against Social Security continues even today. The newspaper *Human Events* tells us that Conservatives want to go back to Dickensonian times. In its December 19, 2003, online edition, one of its contributors, Walter E. Williams, fully illuminates Conservatives' real plans for Social Security:

---

15. Steven F. Hayward, *The Age of Reagan* (Roseville, California: Prima Publishing, 2001), 463.

We all have a moral obligation to pay our share for constitutionally man-dated functions of the federal government, but we have no such obligation to have Congress take the earnings of one American and give them to another American. Forcing one American to serve the purposes of another is one way slavery can be defined.

I'm an emancipated adult fully capable of taking care of my own retire-ment. Why should I or anyone else be forced to pay into the government's Social Security? Do you see any signs on the horizon that such practices are coming to an end? The list of encroachments on personal liberty like these is virtually endless.

Self-determination is a human right we all should respect. If some people want socialism, that's their right—but it is not their right to use brute gov-ernment power to force others, who want liberty, to be a part of it. Liberty-minded Americans might organize to acquire government power to impose their will on socialist-minded Americans, but that's not right either. A far more peaceful method is simply to part company.[16]

Secession? You did not misread that last sentence. The contributor goes on to note that there is a plan in the making, the "Free State Project," for 20,000 people to move to New Hampshire, get as many of them elected as possible to carry out their program of reducing the size of the government and, if they still are forced to cooperate with the federal government, then:

While members of Free State Project have not proposed it, I would imag-ine that if New Hampshire's elected representatives couldn't successfully negotiate with the U.S. Congress to obey the Constitution, the only other alternative would be that of making a unilateral declaration of indepen-dence and go our own way just as our Founders did in 1776.[17]

There you have it. *Human Events* is advocating the same position as Sena-tor Calhoun—nullification. We are back at the cracking point, or perhaps more precisely, the crackpot point.

---

16. Walter E. Williams, "Getting Back Our Liberties," *Human Events Online*, December 19, 2003, at http://www.humaneventsonline.com/article.php?id=2662
17. *Ibid.*

Medicare

The Conservatives opposed Medicare the same way that they opposed Social Security. At the famous Kennedy/Nixon debate in 1960, the two presidential candidates demonstrated their difference of opinion:

> Nixon: Senator Kennedy points out that as far as his one proposal is concerned, the one for medical care for the aged, that that would be financed out of social security. That, however, is raising taxes for those who pay social security.

> Kennedy: Thirdly, on medical care for the aged: This is the same fight that's been going on for 25 years in social security. We wanted to tie it to social security. We offered an amendment to do so; 44 Democrats voted for it; 1 Republican voted for it; and we were informed at the time it came to a vote that if it was adopted the President of the United States would veto it.

> Nixon: The reason why these particular bills in these various fields that have been mentioned were not passed was not because the President was against them; it was because the people were against them. It was because they were too extreme…[18]

Summarizing the Medicare debate at the time, Democratic Senator Henry M. Jackson of Washington appeared on the NBC program "The Campaign and the Candidates" on October 29, 1960, and described the differing Liberal and Conservative viewpoints this way to Moderator Frank McGee:

> Senator JACKSON. Yes, I just want to make this supplementary remark on this particular point; namely, that there's a clear-cut issue here in the area of medical care. The Republicans do not want to place medical care under social security. We in the Democratic Party want it under social security because it treats the rich and the poor alike. We anticipate 10, 15, or 20 years from now, the Republicans will support that program. They opposed social security when it was passed—10, 15, 20 years later, they support it. They are in favor of retroactive progress. I think the record is clear on this.[19]

---

18. "Senator John F. Kennedy and Vice President Richard M. Nixon First Joint Radio-Television Broadcast," *John F. Kennedy Library and Museum*, September 26, 1960, at http://www.jfklibrary.org/60-1st.htm
19. http://www.jfklink.com/speeches/joint/joint291060_nbctv07.html

Senator Jackson was too generous in giving Conservatives credit for favoring "retroactive progress," since they are never in favor of any progress at all. Even when progress has been made—Medicare of the type Senator Jackson was describing was eventually enacted into law—Conservatives try to undo it. As recently as his 2004 State of the Union speech, Bush began to pry out nails holding together Medicare, proposing that:

> By computerizing health records, we can avoid dangerous medical mistakes, reduce costs, and improve care. To protect the doctor-patient relationship, and keep good doctors doing good work, we must eliminate wasteful and frivolous medical lawsuits. And tonight I propose that individuals who buy catastrophic health care coverage, as part of our new health savings accounts, be allowed to deduct 100 percent of the premiums from their taxes.[20]

First, the idea that health care costs are high because of "frivolous lawsuits" is of no merit. Of course any additional cost to a product tends to raise its price, so a frivolous lawsuit has some effect on price. The "frivolous lawsuit" argument is just another attack on the disadvantaged; Conservatives want them to have no remedy against rich doctors and hospitals, so Bush not only blames poor people for the bills sent out by the doctors and hospitals, but he wants to immunize the medical profession from its mistakes. Second, the "health savings account" idea is merely another form of Social Security privatization. Instead of buttressing society's guarantee of adequate health care for the aged, Conservatives want to set up competition for the guarantee and fail to properly fund the guarantee in order to destroy it.

Protections For Working People

American workers' unions have not been islands of innocence in a sea of worldly corruption. The death of Jimmy Hoffa, who will be defended by some forever because of the way he faced down violent opposition by the owners of big industry, may have been the natural consequence of his illegal activities while head of the Teamsters Union.

---

20. "State of the Union Address," *The White House* website, January 20, 2004, at http://www.whitehouse.gov/news/releases/2004/01/20040120-7.html

Can you even imagine a time when the very legality of unions was questioned? Even when considered legal, there was not much in the way of rules by which society could determine the proper role of unions. But this was exactly the shape of things until the Wagner Act was passed under Roosevelt's New Deal in 1935. When introduced for consideration by Senator Wagner of New York, that bill, according to Leuchtenburg:

> [p]roposed to set up a National Labor Relations Board as a permanent independent agency empowered not only to conduct elections to determine the appropriate bargaining units and agents but to restrain business from committing "unfair labor practices" such as discharging workers for union membership or fostering employer-dominated company unions.[21]

For the first time, the federal government agreed that workers could unionize and it began to govern bargaining. Industry then could not refuse to recognize properly organized unions.

You don't have to be a meteorologist to guess which way the Conservative wind blew regarding unions. They were against them, and against their recognition in federal law. Schlesinger notes that one leading newspaper counted the bill as among the most revolutionary ever submitted to Congress, described how leading businessmen denounced the bill as a weapon to impose social coercion that would lead to union leaders controlling American industry, and derided the bill as intended to "out-STALIN Stalin."[22]

The pent-up frustration of the nation's workers with the Conservatives in charge of business life was quickly funneled into union organization. Leuchtenburg recounts how UAW membership skyrocketed from 30,000 to 400,000, how a new union, the SWOC, almost immediately claimed 325,000 members, including the workers at many leading steel companies, and how 450,000 workers in the textile industry, along with other big companies such as General Electric and RCA, were soon unionized.[23]

Let's assume, here in 2004, that illegal activities by union leaders, among other things, have caused union membership to steadily decline in the public sector over the past 30 years, perhaps deservedly so. The point, however, is not whether individual unions have been ill-managed or well-run since the Wag-

---

21. Leuchtenburg, 150-151.
22. *Ibid.*, 404-405.
23. *Ibid.*, 240.

ner Act was passed. If, due to poor management, changing market conditions, or the largess of good business owners, union membership declined at some times, or various other factors caused it to increase at other times, that is just a sign that working people can think for themselves.

As with so many other issues, when the time came for an unequivocal decision, Conservatives lined up on the wrong side because they believe that our federal government, created by the People and codified by the Amended Constitution and with the consent of the governed, is an illegitimate player in the life of the nation. Conservatives simply do not understand our form of national government.

Modernization Of Rural America

As Schlesinger describes, Franklin Roosevelt had an "old absorption with land, forests, and water" and felt by preserving those things, he could redress the imbalance between the city and countryside. Roosevelt's idea was to take kids from city slums and give them the opportunity "for sun and growth in the country," while at the same time allowing for local industries to give part-time work to rural citizens in order to familiarize them with modern society.[24] Although his plan was somewhat utopian, as a Liberal Roosevelt at least had such an absorption. He put it to use in trying to develop the Tennessee River Basin, which comprises parts of seven southern states. In the 60 years or so prior to Roosevelt's election, this land had been ruined by lumbering companies that had decimated the forests and by oil and natural gas companies that had further greatly damaged the area through drilling and mining.[25] This extensive initial damage was followed by the normal complications—"flood, fire, and erosion."[26]

Because of the natural drop-off in the Tennesse River and the consequent turbulence near Muscle Shoals, Alabama, there was great potential power to be garnered from the river. At the time, however, only 2% of the farms there had electricity.[27] Roosevelt wanted to harness the river's power to give electricity to the area and to further the production of nitrates, which were essentials

---

24. Schlesinger, 320.
25. *Ibid.*, at 321.
26. *Ibid.*, at 321.
27. *Ibid.*, at 321.

of both fertilizer and explosives.[28] But Roosevelt wanted to do more than just develop the Muscle Shoals area. Schlesinger outlines Roosevelt's plan:

> Envisioned in its entirety, such use would transcend "mere" power development: it would include flood control, soil conservation, afforestation, diversification of industry and retirement of marginal farm land. To provide unified direction, Roosevelt proposed that Congress create a "corporation clothed with the power of Government but possessed of the flexibility and initiative of private enterprise." The new Tennessee Valley Authority would have "the broadest duty of planning" in the Valley for the general good of the nation.[29]

In the end, the entire area was electrified, figuratively as well as literally. The river was cleared, the forests rebuilt, the soil replenished, agricultural methods improved, schools added, and recreation developed. "The jagged river, flowing uselessly past worn-out fields, overcut forests, ramshackle huts, its muddy waters reflecting the dull poverty of the life around—all this was giving way to a shimmering network of green meadows, blue lakes, and white dams," writes Schlesinger.[30]

The Conservative response to Roosevelt's plans for a TVA was predictable: government was labeled the enemy, and the idea was opposed. Schlesinger continues:

> Congressman Joe Martin of Massachusetts led the Republican attack, declaring that the TVA was "patterned closely after one of the soviet dreams." "No, Mr. Speaker," said Martin, "I think I can accurately predict no one in this generation will see materialize the industrial-empire dream of the Tennessee Valley." "This bill, and every bill like it," said Representative Charles A. Eaton of New Jersey, "is simply an attempt to graft onto our American system the Russian idea."[31]

Conservatives' refusal ever to face down a problem with a solution is as fascinating as it is irresponsible.

---

28. *Ibid.*, 321-323.
29. *Ibid.*, 324.
30. *Ibid.*, 333-334.
31. *Ibid.*, 326.

Despite the obvious success of the TVA, where the powers of government were properly harnessed as providently as that of the river itself, Conservatives never gave up their view that it was all a socialist power grab. When running for President in 1964, Barry Goldwater attacked the TVA. No, he more than attacked it; he advocated selling it to private companies.[32] Of course, it was private companies that had decimated the forests, stripped the land, and let the soil erode in the first place. The Conservative attack on the TVA did not stop with Goldwater. When Reagan ran in the Republican primaries in 1976, he went down the same path. In Tennessee, Reagan mimicked Goldwater, saying that selling off the Tennessee Valley Authority "would be something to look at."[33] So far, the TVA survives, but only because Conservatives have been forced to take the matter off the table because any plan to sell it is so far-fetched. However, when Conservatives get the chance, such as when the government soon becomes so short on cash due to the Bush tax cuts that it will not be able to uphold all of its obligations (Conservatives call this "starving the beast"), Conservatives will serve up this idea once again. You can count on it. We, the People, built the TVA, but when Conservatives have their way, it will be sold to the likes of the men who destroyed the Tennessee Valley in the first place, in a sweetheart deal or deals that experts from Conservative think tanks like the Heritage Foundation will declare fair, and that will be upheld by "strict constructionist" judges appointed by politicians whose campaign coffers were filled by those who will buy them or their allies, and scandal will follow. You can bet on that, too.

Protections For The Environment

Roosevelt's "old absorption with land, forests, and water" encountered more immediate environmental concerns, as well. There was a great drought in 1934 that, in Schlesinger's words, "blighted plains and whirling dust storms darkened western skies."[34] Roosevelt understood, however, that in order to meet these more immediate concerns, there had to be a long-range plan. Roosevelt was concerned because, unlike other leading countries, the U.S. had no national policy for the development of our land and water resources.[35]

---

32. White, 105.
33. Hayward, 472
34. Schlesinger, 335.
35. *Ibid.*, 336.

Roosevelt decided to simultaneously meet the emergency of vast unemployment and the lack of conservation by creating the Civilian Conservation Corps (CCC). Soon, 300,000 men were working in 1300 camps across the country.

Their job was to plant trees, create reservoirs and fish ponds, build dams, dig ditches, raise bridges and fire towers, fight diseases endemic to forests, restore battlefields, clear beaches and camping grounds, and improve parks, forests, watersheds, and recreational areas.[36] Ultimately, 2.5 million people worked in the CCC.[37]

Roosevelt also strengthened the Forest Service. Under his administration, about 200 million trees were planted from Canada to Texas.[38] The idea was to stop another dust bowl from arising by positioning the trees as a huge natural wind break off the Great Plains. It is left to modern science to determine whether this was a success, but two things are true: first, early maps of the U.S. called the Great Plains the "Great American Desert" and, second, we have not had a dust bowl since. In 1935, Congress passed the Soil Conservation Act, the first time that soil conservation hit the national agenda.[39] The Roosevelt Administration also undertook to regulate the excess grazing that had contributed to dust bowl conditions.[40]

In carrying out these programs, Franklin Roosevelt was walking in the deep footsteps of another progressive, Theodore Roosevelt who, in 1905, "launched the conservation movement."[41] Massive undertakings such as the CCC long ago outlived their usefulness and have disbanded. But more modest government programs to protect our land, rivers, and forests have remained in place and even grown.

Regarding all of these environmental matters, our great national debate ran its usual course. With each problem that was identified, Conservatives inevitably said, "Leave it alone—monied capital will fix everything." But capital did not fix anything, not because it inherently works against environmental concerns—robber barons can enjoy a picnic by clean water in clean woods, too, but there was no profit in doing so. Because Capitalism had no incentive to

36. *Ibid.*, 338.
37. *Ibid.*, 339.
38. *Ibid.*, 341.
39. *Ibid.*, 343.
40. *Ibid.*, 346.
41. *Ibid.*, 344.

clean up after itself or to conserve the water and land, it did not. Only a national government dedicated to meeting the problem on a national level could promote environmentalism. Liberals understood this, and it was largely Liberals who saved our country's resources. We all have the choice to be on the right side or the Conservative side of the environment. When informed, Americans choose the correct side, which is the Liberal side.

Protections *For* Business

Ironically from the perspective of Conservatives, who view Liberals as social-ists—or worse—it also was Liberals who saved capitalism. When the Depres-sion hit, banks were folding like bad poker hands confronting a sure full house. The Conservative Hoover administration met this crisis by following a "fiscally conservative" policy of lending banks money to cure their liquidity problem—based, of course, on the banks giving the government "adequate collateral security."[42] The result of applying this Conservative principle to the banking crisis was the closing of all those banks because, as Schlesinger says and any progressive knows, "what the banks needed was not more debt but more capital."[43]

Franklin Roosevelt specifically rejected the advice of some to truly national-ize the banking system; with citizens' confidence at rock bottom, he reached the decision to save the system.[44] He approved a "bank holiday" that closed all banks until confidence could be restored, which due to the "class traitor" Roosevelt's foresight turned out to be only a few days later. Schlesinger observes: "Though technical hitches prevented banks from reopening on Fri-day, March 10, as Roosevelt wished, the basic procedures were nonetheless now established. Gold and deposits were flowing back into the system. After the weekend the people could look forward with assurance to orderly reopen-ing."[45]

Later, the Roosevelt administration formed the Reconstruction Finance Corporation, which purchased $1 billion more preferred stock in banks that badly needed it.[46] Roosevelt also formed the Federal Deposit Insurance Cor-

---

42. *Ibid.*, 426.
43. *Ibid.*, 426.
44. *Ibid.*, 5.
45. *Ibid.*, 8.
46. *Ibid.*, 430.

poration, which insures almost all bank deposits in this country up to $100,000 each. This federal agency helped further to save the banking system and thus capitalism. Average citizens became confident that, when they gave their money to the capitalist to hold, they would actually get it back. The *federal* government guarantee "collateralized" the capitalist's word, thereby giving it the credibility it lacked standing alone.

I have served on the Board of Directors of two national banks, one for about a decade. The heads of both those banks—one my father, and the other a dear friend later in life—often complained about the federal "regulators" paying their periodic visits to the institutions. Nobody likes being watched. Yet both those men deeply understood the necessity of such oversight and FDIC insurance as part of the same package of public confidence-building measures without which they well might not have had their banks at all. As for me, I was always thankful that an unbiased group of people who thoroughly understood banking kept their eyes on things no matter what my personal relationship was with the heads of the banks. Checks and balances, as American as apple pie, are the only way to ensure that all parties fulfill their duties to everyone.

Roosevelt supplied lifeblood as well to other new federal agencies for capitalism's heart to pump. Schlesinger describes the formation of the Commodity Credit Corporation, which supported agriculture through loans and storage facilities; the Electric Home and Farm Authority, which assisted rural electrification with consumer loans for electrical appliances; the RFC Mortgage Company and the Federal National Mortgage Association, which worked with the Federal Housing Administration to create a badly needed mortgage market; the Export-Import Bank, whose purpose was to stimulate trade; and other programs to pay teachers' salaries, lend money to railroads, keep down interest rates, provide assistance to victims of natural disasters, and make loans to mining and gas companies, airlines, and construction firms.[47]

Perhaps American Conservatives cannot be blamed for the Depression, given that the world ran out of money in the aftermath of World War I by hanging onto the "Gold Standard," which tied the supply of money to the amount of gold in the world. Thus, when the supply of gold became insufficient—which was inevitable as human population growth drove up general demand for goods and services—the world economy could not grow. For a

---

47. *Ibid.*, 430.

Conservative, Hoover did all he could stomach to involve the federal government in helping to solve the problem. But while the patient needed a tourniquet, all Hoover would supply was a better form of band-aid. On the other hand, American Conservatives were part of the *Weltanschauung* of all Conservatives at the time, which linked our economy to the Gold Standard in the first place. This tied a big gold weight to America's foot and threw it overboard.

Liberals did not only save our banking, mortgage, railroad, mining, smelting, and agricultural systems; they also fixed the infrastructure and wired rural America for electricity. Conservatives might forget this when they stop at a motel in rural Georgia and find that there actually is a motel—not only because the owners got a mortgage to buy it, but also because electrical wires were laid so that management can cook the food and provide the traveler with lights and heat.

And it doesn't stop there. Liberals also saved the financial markets, previously loosely called "the Stock Market." These markets were saved the same way banking was—by giving the capitalist system credibility. Although the Depression was not caused by fraud, once it started the entire capitalist system was called into question, and the fraud endemic to that system and all other human-made systems might have been the straw that really did break its back. Liberals met this challenge when the Roosevelt administration developed the Securities and Exchange Commission, the Securities Act of 1933, and the Securities Exchange Act of 1934 (and subsequent supplemental Acts). These laws put the raising of any sort of sizeable money through the sale of stock or other securities under Uncle Sam's watchful eyes, with severe penalties for their fraudulent or, in some cases, inadvertent breach. Conservatives have never stopped arguing that the laws were unnecessary, since they haven't stopped the incidence of fraud, but that's not the point. In today's world, investors at least know that the crooked securities dealers of the country will have to face federal music and do federal time which, combined with federal oversight to begin with, gives the investor community enough confidence to lay its money on the table, thereby helping to ensure that capitalism will work.

The Conservative "thank-you" for saving American capitalism was an offensive to convince the American public that Franklin Roosevelt and his administration were out to destroy America. Schlesinger reports that the:

> *Commercial and Financial Chronicle*...concluded that this would mean "a class dictatorship to which all would have to submit and from the rule of

which no one could escape...the extinction of freedom. The image of the New Deal, as it emerged from these writings was that of the totalitarian state—in the words of Ogden Mills, "an all-powerful central government to which all men must look for security, guidance and assistance, and which, in turn, undertakes to control and direct the lives and destinies of all."[48]

Reprising their States' Rights tune, Conservatives also attacked the new Deal as intending to "abolish the sovereignty of the States." Next, Conservatives compared Roosevelt to mass-murdering dictators, accusing him "of centralized order-giving...[that] more strongly resembles the dictatorship of the Fascistic and Communist states of Europe than it does the American system."[49] The modern attacks on Liberals are difficult to understand. In return for putting nearly everybody on the business team, business and Conservatives responded by calling the plan "dictatorship." What an insult to the millions of hungry, homeless, unemployed men and women who, in exchange for the promise that they would not be considered merely a human commodity, stood *with* the American business system. If not for these Liberal reforms to save the whole country, American business people might indeed have faced dictatorship and, if they had, would have soon seen the difference between their Liberal saviors and a dictator's jack-booted minions. We can add short-sightedness to the list of Conservative shortcomings.

Two National Problems, Two Solutions

As history shows, then, virtually every government service we take for granted was created by Liberals and opposed at its inception by Conservatives, whose "arguments" against each consisted of a call for States' Rights and name calling as Marxist or fascist. However, memorization of historical details is less important than the ability to critically assess why being a Liberal in today's society is not only important but necessary, as a discussion of our most challenging issues in 2004, universal health care (UHC) and education, will show.

Universal Health Care

For Liberals, the solution to UHC is easy—the country must have it. Conservatives will respond: "socialism," "communism," the end of "federalism."

---

48. *Ibid.*, 472-473.
49. *Ibid.*, 473.

These responses are—as they were when Hillary Clinton pushed for UHC—simply inadequate and inhumane. The question is not whether the United States needs UHC; it is which plan to implement. Conservatives will again roll their eyes, saying, "First, you made us ensure that everyone had enough food, then you made us try to give everybody a place to sleep, next you made us provide everybody a few pennies in old age, and then you said we had to help old people pay for some of their medication. Now you want us to provide everyone with health care, too?" Yes, that is exactly what Liberals want.

Conservatives are correct about one thing: an old, Bulgarian-style UHC plan will only remind us of, well, Bulgaria, and maybe Jimmy Carter. Hillary's plan would have created a monster bureaucracy that in the end would have been self-defeating—because while everyone would have had a theoretical right to health care, the competitive system that has fostered great scientific advancement might be lost in the process. We need to do something that harnesses medicine's legitimate capitalistic instincts—the desire of doctors and hospitals to make a lot of money—for the good of the people. We cannot justify neglecting this any longer. There is simply no reason why when some of us are sick or injured, we have insurance to pay the bill, while others of us do not. People do not learn so-called Conservative values such as individual initiative by dying at 15 for lack of health care.

Health care in this country is built around a good theoretical idea that doesn't work very well in reality—health insurance. In a normal capitalistic society, citizens pay for what they purchase. If they want the Lexus, they pay a Lexus price, but if they will settle for the beater Chevy, the price is a lot less. In either case, the price and car are connected.

Imagine, however, that instead of the automobile insurance we ordinarily have, "car insurance" meant that a company receiving a monthly premium would buy a car whenever the contributor decided it was "needed." Just about everyone would purchase the Lexus, and the price of the Lexus, already high, would climb precipitously year after year. That may sound far-fetched, but that is exactly how health insurance works. One pays a premium, and then when one "needs" the health care, the insurance company, not the customer, pays for the care. Not surprisingly, the price of health care continues to climb precipitously. The only difference between health care and the Lexus is that the price of the Lexus would rise faster, because one would tend to "need" it more, because one would want it more. It's more fun to drive a Lexus than have to be driven to the doctor.

The health care industry blames higher costs on an aging population, frivolous doctor visits, medical care fraud, and a number of other factors. These may have some effect, but they all dodge the real cause—which is that there is no connection between the pocket of individual Americans and health care. Rather, some far-away entity called "an insurance company," an "HMO," or a "PPO" pays the bill. If government paid the bill directly, the effect would probably be pretty similar, and possibly even less efficient. At least in the current system, competing companies try to be creative. If government paid the bill, the basic problem of a third-party payor driving up the price would not change, but there would be no competition. A single bureaucracy—a governmental one—would replace the various private firms. The system would necessarily be more rigid because a monopoly would control all health care and there would be only one set of "fair" rules.

So, we should try to improve the current system, with its advantages of the inherent efficiencies of the healthcare marketplace—and existing government bureaucracy—rather than create a new behemoth. We can do this by continuing to have private health insurance and its HMO and PPO cousins provide the majority of health care funds, while designating the federal government the insurer of last resort. Most of the government work can be done by the Internal Revenue Service (IRS) and the Department of Health and Human Services (HHS), as follows.

HHS can break down the American population into actuarially appropriate demographic categories, such as age and sex. HHS can then qualify insurance companies to bid to insure any or all of the designated groups. The term of the contract will be the period of time that HHS determines is appropriate to encourage competition, while keeping in mind that a turnover in companies could lead to bottlenecks in providing coverage and services for each designated group. HHS will approve the contracts from the companies that submit the lowest and best premium bid. HHS may sub-divide the designated groups as to size, to ensure that a company can handle the number of people in the group. Most Americans will be identified in one or another designated insurance group on their tax returns either as filers or dependents. Within 60 days of April 15, each year, the winning insurance company for each group or sub-group will receive from the U.S. Treasury a check for each group member's pro-rata share of the bid-for premium, and each group member will have private health insurance. The experts and Congress can decide what kind of a tax, if any, to impose (straight pro-rata would amount to a flat tax, so it may have to be graduated), and how to lessen its burden of any tax, by having the federal government collect as additional revenues those monies that previously would have been used to pay health insurance premiums. In this way it would be pretty much a wash as to cost for the insured as compared with the present system.

The implementation of this plan hinges on the filing of tax returns. Everyone who wants to be covered will have to file a return. Those who would not have to file a tax return—because they do not earn enough income, for example—would simply check a box indicating that no financial information is required. Because even criminals deserve medical care, if someone who is avoiding filing a return because it will incriminate him or her, that person can check a separate, "no questions asked" box.

This should enable just about everyone to become insured, while increasing the income of insurance companies that offer the best insurance at the best price, and, thereby, also possibly increasing private employment. However, some people will still be out of the loop for one reason or another. When such people are discovered—a disabled elderly person or one who does not speak English—the insurance company providing the policy will cover them. If the number of people for whom coverage is ultimately provided exceeds the number estimated in the bid, the insurance company will be paid an extra premium by the federal government. If someone is found not to fit into any insured group but is in need of treatment, the government will pay the bill. Congress will decide if certain groups, such as undocumented foreign workers, are covered, but that likely will be subject to courts' similar decisions in matters such as Social Security and public education as to whether such people may be excluded from government benefits.

Because the President has concluded that deficits don't matter, we can implement this system in five years after building a trust fund of however much Congress decides to prepare for the extra costs.

Though some of the details of this plan are flexible, by taking a lesson from the system of checks and balances invented by this nation's Founders, we can confidently assume that Congress will pass a UHC system soon. We can keep all the politicians honest, both Liberal and Conservative, and ensure the best UHC system with the following rule: The President, Supreme Court Justices, and all members of Congress will have to give up their current personal health care and enter the system they approve for everyone else. When those in Washington share the same health care with secretaries, machinists, toll booth operators, and even the homeless, they'll find a way to make it work.

Education

Conservatives have proposed actual solutions, be they good or bad, to two national problems out of all those this country has faced since its founding, and both concerned education. First, Texas Conservatives countered affirmative action by enacting a law automatically admitting the top 10% of every Texas high school's graduating class to the Texas state universities. Although that solution has been criticized by Liberals for perpetuating segregated schools, the fact is that schools *are* segregated. If they were not, that would indicate that racism was pretty much gone, so the "10% solution" would not be needed anyway. As things stand now, even if the rich, white suburban kid is in the upper 10% of the class with higher board scores or grades than the kid who went to a "bad" urban school, s/he may have a tougher time in college just because the city kid did well despite having the deck stacked against him or her. Groundbreaking or not, and ultimately able to redress the problem or not, this solution was creative and represents the type of alternatives Conservatives should be offering rather than always obstructing progress.

The Conservatives' other educational idea—vouchers—has a certain surface appeal and has even attracted approval from an unlikely source—African-Americans. Some polls put African-American support of vouchers at between 59% and 72%.[50] Reporter Peter Schrag recounts the development of the idea, and the role George W. Bush played:

> President Bush told an intimate audience in Washington Thursday that he stands behind his campaign pledge to give parents more ability to remove their children from unsafe or academically inadequate public schools.
>
> Such ability, he said, could be in the form of school vouchers, a hot-button issue among Democrats and some educators.
>
> Bush told those assembled in an Eisenhower Executive Office Building auditorium he was "strongly committed" to shifting federal money directly to parents if the schools their children attend cannot meet the standards set by local officials....

---

50. Peter Schrag, "The Voucher Seduction," *The American Prospect Online*, November 23, 1999, at http://www.prospect.org/print_friendly/print/ V11/1/schrag_p.html

Vouchers, or cash disbursements to parents of children attending schools rated as failures, could be used to enroll those children in another school, public or private.

Democrats oppose the idea, saying such payments would siphon sorely needed money from the schools that may need it the most.

Bush's proposal would divert to a child's parents—at least on paper—federal money that would have gone to a school system for the same child.

When he campaigned for the presidency last year, Bush suggested that could come to $1,500 per year for parents to enroll their children on another public school, a charter school, or a private establishment....

"If a failing school does not change after a period of time," Bush said, "parents should be able to take the federal money attributable to their child...and make a choice of any school they want to send that child to"...

"We need to empower parents by giving them more options and influence," he said.

The Bush education overhaul agenda is based on his insistence on local control over curriculum and spending. Bush has called for a spending regime that would allow localities to spend federal money as they see fit....

He also said schools that do not improve internal safety for their students could face sharp declines in their student population if, as he would like, parents are allowed to transfer their children. The states, he said, would be responsible for certifying how safe their schools are.

"Students in unsafe schools must be given the option to attend another public school," he said.[51]

At first blush, this doesn't sound too bad. If the local schools are not doing their jobs, they "get fired" by their consumers, the public. However, the voucher idea stems from the same illegitimate "philosophy" as virtually every other Conservative domestic "solution"—an attempt to relieve government of its proper concerns for all "the People." Vouchers are not really Conservatives' way to whip public schools into shape by making them compete. Rather, the

---

51. Ian Christopher McCaleb, "Bush Pushes for School Vouchers," *CNN.com*, April 12, 2001, at http://www.cnn.com/2001/ ALLPOLITICS/04/12/bush.speech/index.html

basic idea behind school vouchers is to destroy the public school system entirely. Just as Social Security is not meant to compete in the retirement income market because it is a guarantee of a minimum income for the elderly, not an investment, so public education is not meant to compete in the education market because it, too, is a guarantee—of a minimum education for the young:

> One thread that pulls all of this together is an economic thread; private school vouchers for some people are based not on a religious idea, but on an economic idea, primarily due to the thinking of a free-market economist named Milton Friedman, who proposed taxpayer-supported vouchers in 1954. Friedman wanted to get government out of the provision of education altogether. For him, vouchers funded by taxpayers were a transition to doing that. Under his conception, the government would provide a minimum education grant, in the form of a voucher for each child, and parents could then use those funds to send their child to any educational institution they wished: secular, nonsectarian, religious—any sort of educational institution.[52]

The "man behind modern school vouchers" (with thanks to his mentors-in-spirit, Adam Smith and Thomas Paine) is Milton Friedman, the Nobel Prize winning economist from the University of Chicago. Friedman really is a deep thinker, he is not a racist, and his public persona always has been that of a kind man. Analyzed on a simple market economic model, there is some validity to the Friedman-Conservative model. However, even based simply on the market, vouchers present problems. For instance, say that every parent in New York State receives $7,500 per year per child. That $7,500 will not buy the same thing in a depressed urban area as in a suburb. The suburban school districts will still tax their residents and pay higher salaries to their teachers. This will continue to drain talent from the depressed areas. Certainly, Conservatives will not allow the evil federal government to tell local governments they cannot tax to gain a competitive advantage. The same $7,500 will not buy in the depressed area what it does in the more affluent area also because the

---

52. Alex Molnar, "The Case Against Vouchers," *Freethought Today*, November 1996, at http://www.ffrf.org/fttoday/nov96/molnar.html. This is excerpted from a speech presented at the national convention of the Freedom From Religion Foundation in Madison, Wisconsin, on October 12, 1996.

infrastructure in the affluent areas will continue to be much better than the depressed areas, thereby again attracting talent away from the depressed areas.

The Conservatives urge "not to worry" because with money in their pockets for education, the otherwise poor parents will have the resources to send their kids to the more attractive schools, or new schools will be started in the depressed areas to take in all that new money in the local pockets. Neither will happen. Some astute business person can figure out how to send office products or soybeans from one area to another less expensively from a farther distance than from a closer business because of one competitive advantage or another. Somebody else will always figure out how to send a shipment of soybeans from Iowa to Florida cheaper than from a closer point and still make money, and the market will follow. But children are not office products, they are not soy beans, they are not any commodity at all. Indeed, even though the spirit behind it was fine, '70s-style "busing" failed to achieve integration for the same reason. We can ship our children only so far every morning, and it isn't very far. Moreover, even with the tuition money in their pockets, poor parents simply won't have the additional funds to send their kids traipsing off to somebody else's better school. The affluent kids will then have a big advantage: they will go home a short distance away, take a nap, and get on with their homework. The poor kids will come home bedraggled and worn out from the long commute, with less time for homework. Furthermore, to the extent that the kids are of working age, the poor ones won't be able to go to their jobs, or might have to start them even later each day. One way poor kids have tried to compete is through athletics. But even if vouchers otherwise work, they will place these students at another disadvantage, because the commuting will cut into their practice and game time as well. And there will be other unforeseen financial issues. The poor kids will beg their parents for their last dime to buy some fancy brand that the rich kids already have, putting more pressure on an already strapped family.

Neither will there be a mad rush to start and build competitive schools in poorer neighborhoods. There will be some success stories, to be sure, where particularly bright and hardworking private urban educators tailor their schools to the community's needs and run them at a good profit while providing quality education. But, in general, poor neighborhoods will not be able to compete with more affluent ones for the same reason there are fewer nice houses, nice cars, and nice appliances in poor neighborhoods than rich ones: those things are commodities, and when we turn schools into commodities they are going to go to the same place as all the others—to where the money is, which is where the rich people are. So, the rich will get better educated and richer forever under vouchers, which is of course the Conservatives' goal. Moreover, partial success for a voucher system would spell disaster for the public schools; if vouchers did not entirely replace the public school system, we would be left with a public school system more or less crippled in inverse proportion to the success of the voucher system. Then, either school districts would default, a disaster for schools and their creditors alike, or Conservatives would be faced with their favorite entertainment—a tax hike.

But, mostly, Liberals should oppose vouchers because, like other Conservative ideas, a voucher program is intended to break government's longstanding commitment to providing a fundamental service to its citizens. Without a properly educated citizenry, our country will not survive as a democracy. Here is what Horace Mann, the founder of modern education, had to say on the subject:

> Now surely nothing but universal education can counterwork this tendency to the domination of capital and the servility of labor. If one class possesses all the wealth and the education, while the residue of society is ignorant and poor, it matters not by what name the relation between them may be called: the latter, in fact and in truth, will be the servile dependents and subjects of the former. But, if education be equally diffused, it will draw property after it by the strongest of all attractions; for such a thing never did happen, and never can happen, as that an intelligent and practical body of men should be permanently poor. Property and labor in different classes are essentially antagonistic; but property and labor in the same class are essentially fraternal. The people of Massachusetts have, in some degree, appreciated the truth that the unexampled prosperity of the State—its comfort, its competence, its general intelligence and virtue—is attributable to the education, more or less perfect, which all its people have received; but are they sensible of a fact equally important—namely, that it is to this same education that two-thirds of the people are indebted for not being to-day the vassals of as severe a tyranny, in the form of capital, as the lower classes of Europe are bound to in any form of brute force?
>
> Education then, beyond all other devices of human origin, is a great equalizer of the conditions of men,—the balance wheel of the social machinery. I do not here mean that it so elevates the moral nature as to make men disdain and abhor the oppression of their fellow men. This idea pertains to another of its attributes. But I mean that it gives each man the independence and the means by which he can resist the selfishness of other men. It does better than to disarm the poor of their hostility toward the rich: it prevents being poor.[53]

These words were delivered by Mann in 1848. Conservatives are frightened by socialists, communists, and other agitators. As Mann was perhaps suggesting, Conservatives would do well to remember that Europe was torn by mighty (and mighty dangerous) revolutions in 1848, and perhaps the best way to avert such events is to make sure all our citizens have a stake in the organization, a necessary component of which is a proper basic public education.

There is only one way to attack the education problem in the United States, and that is seriously. Nobody seems to want to do that, including most Liberals. Even the Clinton administration failed to improve public education a whit. It takes money and human resources to invest in education.

Liberals prefer the term "investment" to "taxes." In many cases, that's mealy-mouthing. But when it comes to education, there really is an investment aspect. Society will not succeed without cultivating our children's minds. We will have to be patient and we will have to admit that we need taxes for education, and a lot of them. And here it is not a matter of anything except prioritizing. Let us, for example, consider what the $87 billion voted by Congress in 2003 to be used for Iraq's reconstruction could have brought in the reconstruction of public education: With $87 billion, we could build brand new schools for almost 7 million students at the price per student of Jeb Bush's Florida, or roughly 2 million students at the price per student of Arnold Schwarzenegger's California.[54] And that's just what Bush has planned for Iraq in the first year. If some Liberal had stood up in the United States Senate (as s/he should have) and advocated spending $87 billion on schools, that Senator would have been laughed off the floor by Trent Lott and friends, and Bush would have been yelling, "tax and spend" at every news conference.[55]

---

53. "Horace Mann on Education And National Welfare 1848 (Twelfth Annual Report of Horace Mann as Secretary of Massachusetts State Board of Education)," *TnCrimLaw*, at http://www.tncrimlaw.com/ civil_bible/horace_mann.htm

54. "School Building Costs: Public vs. Private," *School Reform News*, January 1, 2002, republished by *Heartland Institute*, at http://www. heartland.org/Article.cfm?artId=247

55. For $87 billion dollars, the Small Business Administration could also make 174,000 loans of $50,000 each to create jobs in depressed areas. That's just another way of looking at that bit of pocket change being shipped overseas.

The best way, therefore, to attract Conservatives other than rich contractors to our own rebuilding effort is to address some of the Conservatives' valid concerns while making education the priority it so desperately needs and deserves to be. One Conservative objection has to do with Liberals' frequent inability to acknowledge that a gunshot within earshot of a school can have a negative effect on the learning process. Instead of the 100,000 more cops Bill Clinton claims to have put on the street, we should create "crime-free zones" around schools. Put however many squad cars as necessary within a 1-mile radius or so of every school that has a "crime problem" during the school day and a reasonable after-school period. We'll get the money back in the long term by having to build fewer prisons and guard fewer prisoners. Or are Conservatives frightened that those who would otherwise end up as prisoners might not vote with them if they received the education to make them good citizens? Certainly our greatest concern should be to make schools and their surrounding areas so safe that the biggest fear even poor urban kids have on their way to school is wondering if Spot has received his rabies shot. Go ahead, put a couple of former Green Berets in each school as the truant/disciplinary officers, too. Getting it done will get it over with sooner, rather than later, so that the extra officers aren't even needed anymore.

Next, we need a major public relations campaign at least as strong as the one for the War on Terror to get everybody in on the act. The President of the United States has to inspire the Senate and House Education Committees to come up with a real bipartisan plan to utilize the full force of the government to encourage careers in education, teach parents and children the value of staying in school, provide modern facilities, and keep those facilities safe. If all the politicians in Washington, in consultation with all the biggest and/or brightest advertising companies in the country, cannot come up with a way to motivate kids and their parents or other caretakers to value and complete their basic education, then all advertising dollars may as well be re-routed to cigarettes.

Of course, Conservatives won't carry out this game plan, because they do not really want the level playing field they claim to hold in such high regard. They hold back sufficient funding and discipline because they are afraid that when there is real competition, their kids won't come out on top. Both Liberals and Conservatives understand that an educated population is the key to democracy. That is why Conservatives are trying to destroy public education and divide us into the educated and non-educated, and Liberals are trying to preserve it. This attitude is consistent with the Conservatives' entire history of dividing the country.

Reason 4. Liberals Support Religion's Humanitarian Principles.

As with other issues, Conservatives use religion to divide the country rather than unite it. It seems implicit in the Conservatives' names for their organizations—"the Moral Majority" for example—that they think they have a monopoly on G-d. This does demonstrate a certain consistency in Conservative thought, as Conservatives are fond of monopolies. However, Conservatives want to put into public life only the more ritualistic aspects of religion—such as the mere act of going to church or putting up a creche in a public square on Christmas—in which the government has no interest, rather than religion's social concerns, in which the government has a similar, though distinct, interest.

Ritual has a respectable place in religion, as nationalism does in political life, but each goes only so far. They are bound together in the same package by Conservatives, because they are the easiest parts of religion and patriotism, respectively, to grasp. Various religious rituals unify congregants. The act of repeating the Pledge of Allegiance, with or without the G-d part, unifies our citizens. Study hard the meaning of the rituals, which most people don't, and it is possible to make more out of ritual. Study the words of the Pledge, which most people don't, and we can make something out of that, too (namely, a big disappointment for Conservatives, since the Pledge requires liberty and justice for all—from the government, no less—because that's what the *flag* represents, of course).

Many Liberals believe that religion has no role to play in our liberal, democratic system of government. They are mistaken.[1] The right wing should not

95

take too much heart in those words, however, because religion's role is not to authorize prayer in school (what's stopping anyone from thinking a prayer in the first place?) or to start school-sponsored football games with a huddle where the players are encouraged to pray collectively. Such requirements are highly offensive to non-believers and different-believers, and we should have zero tolerance for them. On the other hand, there is no problem with any member of the clergy giving a speech at a graduation ceremony, making religious references, and talking about how religion affected him or her, or even hearing such things from the President—Lincoln certainly included religion in the Gettysburg Address. However, these matters should be referred to by the speaker as a personal opinion or experience, not as government policy.

The proper place for religion in public life is to influence public policy—as carried out by government—through the universal humanitarian principles enumerated by religion. This is the religion Conservatives fear, because it is consistent with Lincoln and Roosevelt's reformations of our society, which means actually utilizing the government we formed for good purposes, rather than declaring our own creation of an enemy non-combatant. We Liberals need to start selling religion's proper role in creating a *just* society concerned with helping the disadvantaged, because like almost everything Liberal, it is simply a better product, with much wider appeal, than its Conservative competition.

Mainly, the goal of the fundamentalist Conservatives is to impose their personal moral code upon all society. Equating one's personal code with good public policy is not a wise idea. It shows no respect for others' personal codes and is contrary to our concept of separating church and state. Certainly, any Liberal who thinks common standards of right and wrong have no value in public life is delusional, but in general Liberals have the much stronger case in asserting that the public arena is the place where we decide our public questions of right and wrong, not our private ones. If we follow the Conservative path, our public debates will focus on unresolvable—and therefore divi-

---

1. Nor will our Republic fall due to the appearance of the words, "in G-d we trust," on our money (quite a place for that phrase, considering certain money changers' problems when they came face-to-face with religion personified), or even the words, "under G-d," in the Pledge of Allegiance, although neither phrase is really appropriate under the Constitution.

sive—private issues, as indicated by Jerry Falwell's own web page concerning the Supreme Court's striking down the Texas anti-sodomy law:

> (AgapePress)—In his letter to the Romans, the apostle Paul says men whose "foolish hearts were darkened" exchanged the truth of God for a lie. His warning about man's wisdom has apparently gone unheeded in Washington, D.C., where the U.S. Supreme Court has struck down an anti-sodomy law in Texas—effectively telling states they can no longer punish homosexual couples for engaging in activities the Bible says are "unnatural" and sinful....

> "Today's decision represents yet another instance of the Court not merely declaring the law, but actually making it," says Crampton, who had argued that issues of morality are under the authority of states, not the federal courts. [According to Steve Crampton, chief counsel for the American Family Association's Center for Law & Policy.]

> Appearing on CNN, Rob Schenck of the National Clergy Council says today's decision means the courts no longer recognize immoral behavior.

> "The fact is that homosexual behavior is immoral—it is wrong," Schenck says. "And what the court has said today is that right and wrong—morality versus immorality—no longer matters in the law. That is wrong. It undermines our concept of justice and it demoralizes our culture."[2]

This Conservative fundamentalist viewpoint is now familiar. From the time Jefferson Davis failed to see the connection between the chains he wore after the Civil War and the chains of his slaves to more recent Conservative attacks on homosexual rights, the problem has remained constant.

Matters at the core of the various religions' belief systems—such as whether there is a trinity; whether transubstantiation is a literal fact, a symbol of a past fact, or not something to believe on any level; matters of eschatology; whether miracles literally occurred or never happened; and whether Muhammad was the last prophet or no prophet at all—have no place in the public discussion. Thus, the decision to accept or reject Christianity's main theological proposition of Jesus as one's personal savior is a purely personal matter having no relevance to our earthly government's policies.

---

2.   Sherrie Black, Allie Martin, and Jody Brown, "High Court Strikes Down Texas Sodomy Law," *Agape Press*, June 26, 2003, at http://headlines.agapepress.org/archive/6/262003a.asp and republished at http://www.falwell.com

On the other hand, the *humanitarian* lessons of religion, although spring-ing perhaps from a more noble purpose than the self-interest underlying the original social contract, have an altogether useful and necessary place in the public debate. A Christian's duties to the poor, the incarcerated, and the dis-abled may be applied in the public arena in addition to the private. Jesus's the-ology in this regard is explained by UCC Justice and Witness Ministries at its website, www.Jesus-Institute.org:

> Jesus had a special sense of mission to poor and oppressed people. At the outset of his ministry, sometimes referred to as Jesus' mission statement, Jesus stood up in the synagogue at Nazareth and read from the prophet Isa-iah:
>
> "The Spirit of the Lord is on me, because he has anointed me to preach good news to the poor. He has sent me to proclaim freedom for the prison-ers and recovery of sight for the blind, to release the oppressed, to proclaim the year of the Lord's favor." (Luke 4:18-19)
>
> The biographies of Jesus depict him repeatedly reaching out to those at the bottom of the social pyramid—poor people, women, Samaritans, lepers, children, prostitutes and tax collectors. Jesus was also eager to accept people who were well-placed, but he made clear that all, regardless of social posi-tion, needed to repent. For this reason, he invited the rich young man to sell all of his possessions and give the proceeds to the poor. (Matthew 19:16-30, Luke 18:18-30, Mark 10:17-31)
>
> Jesus commanded, "Love your neighbor." When asked to define "neigh-bor," Jesus expanded the traditional meaning of the word—defining our neighbor as anyone who is in need, including social outcasts: "But when you give a banquet, invite the poor, the crippled, the lame, the blind, and you will be blessed." (Luke 14:13)[3]

This only true relation of religion to politics has been eloquently detailed by Bob Rae, the former Premier of Ontario Province, Canada, who demonstrates that a government truly applying religious principles is the one that takes care of the weak, not the one that tries to impose one person's rituals or concepts of G-d on anybody else:

---

3.   "Jesus the Advocate for the Poor," from J. Bennett Guess, "Biblical Foundations for Justice Advocacy," UCC Justice and Witness Minis-tries, adapted by *Jesus Institute*, at http://www.jesus-institute.org/life-of-jesus-modern/jesus-poor.shtml

Rabbi Hillel, who lived in Babylon more than 2,000 years ago once questioned: If I am not for myself, who is for me? But if I am only for myself, what am I? And if not now, when? The first question points to the enduring value of self-interest, which we ignore at our peril; the second to the need for generosity and justice in a world that values greed too much; the third speaks to the need for action and the danger of doing nothing, a vice to which we are all, in our private and public moments, too prone.

The pursuit of self-interest in the economy is as natural for the trade unionist as it is for the entrepreneur or even tycoon. The healthy competition of the market, and the achievement of our own individual success is not to be scorned or feared. Economic and political systems that do not attach a priority to the satisfaction of this demand from individuals have failed and will continue to fail. Prosperity matters. Billie Holiday reminded the world that I have been poor and have been rich, and rich is better…

…But to assert self-interest is not enough, which is why Hillel asked his second question: But if I am only for myself, what am I? The trouble with brash neo-conservatives, excessive nationalists, and single-issue politicians alike is that they all stop with the assertion of self-interest. Their obsession with self keeps them from coming to terms with the second questions.…

…Social democracy must change so that it can once again become a healthy and realistic public philosophy. We should be setting stronger rules for markets, and recognizing that while not everything is for sale, innovation, technological change and the fundamental importance of education have everything to do with the creation of wealth. We should not be ashamed of seeking prosperity.

But a prosperity that is too confined and exclusive begins to take on its own pathology. The rich hardly give away enough money to make up for the relative decline in tax revenues and government expenditure. This means poorer schools, a weakened health-care system, and social services for children and the vulnerable that have gone from barely adequate to impoverished.[4]

This is the essence of Liberalism. That Conservatives berate Liberals for modernizing the collection of food, clothing, shelter, and medical attention through the auspices of the nation state, otherwise known as taxation, rather

---

4.   Bob Rae, "21st Century Citizenship Working Group Report," *Policy Network*, 2003, at http://www.progressive-governance.net/php/article.php?sid=4&aid=194

than relying upon the good will of private citizens is beyond comprehension. Moreover, the Conservatives' belittling of these efforts is decidedly anti-religious. We Liberals need to take this message to the people, because to my way of thinking, feeding the poor is a lot more important to G-d than intoning the words, "under G-d" in a rote babbling that demeans the holy by equating G-d with the profane—a mere worldly government.[5]

Unlike the Moral Majority, or other current and former Conservative fund-raising front groups, Liberals will never say that G-d is on their side. Nobody knows if refusing to engage in or tolerate sodomy (or engaging in it with a committed partner) is a surer way to get into heaven than feeding and clothing the poor. But this much is true: the former concerns personal conduct in which the government has no business. The latter is the government's business whether or not it is religion's, and to the extent Liberals can promote it by drawing on their and others' religious experiences, they should.

---

5.   The Conservatives make the same error in their endless desire to pass a flag-burning Amendment to the Constitution or a law that will ban that activity, which they label a "desecration" of the flag. The only "desecration" going on in that effort is by the Conservatives, because equating any human symbol, even Old Glory, with "desecration"—a religious term—is idolatry. Now, idolatry is legal, too, but let's make it clear who are the idolaters. It isn't the Liberals.

Reason 5. Liberals Support a United Military Representing A United People.

Nowhere is the Conservatives' attempt to divide our country more evident than in foreign relations. Our greatest warrior-Presidents have been Liberals. Lincoln took the time in the middle of his war to liberate the slaves from our oligarchic, semi-feudal, Conservative South. Wilson led us to victory in World War I. Franklin Roosevelt defeated both the Empire of Japan and Nazi Germany. Truman fought the communist governments of Russia and China to a standstill in Korea against overwhelming odds and otherwise stood fast in the Cold War (while at the same time upholding the principle of civilian control over the military by sacking General Douglas MacArthur, an autocratic "man on horseback" whom the Conservatives wanted to rule over our country—preferably after nuking China). Kennedy and Johnson, however unwisely, undertook our involvement in Vietnam. In fact, the Liberals' resolute engagement with the rest of the world led Conservatives to mount attacks such as this one of Bob Dole's in a vice-presidential debate with Walter Mondale in 1976: "If we added up the killed and wounded in Democrat wars in this century, it'd be about 1.6 million Americans, enough to fill the city of Detroit." And, yet, for all the Liberals' resoluteness and even ferocity in the face of foreign threats, Conservatives have spent the past century blasting Liberals as disloyal Fifth Columnists for America's enemies. Given the Conservatives' traditional isolationism, not to mention their secession from the Union and the donning of the uniform of an enemy nation, these charges of disloyalty are a particularly dishonest way for Conservatives to gain political power. "Dishonest" is a good word for it, because in this way, Conservatives copy the tactic of "the big lie" developed by the German fascists, who were real enemies of America.

Hitler's thesis was that every lie contains within it a kernel of truth, and that therefore telling a "big lie" was more effective than telling a small one, because if proportionately the same percentage of every lie remains in the human consciousness, in absolute terms, there is always more left over from the big lie than a little one.[1] Who knows whether the mind really works that way, but his approach seems to have succeeded in one important instance that has greatly influenced American Conservatives: the "Reichstag Fire."

The fire at the Reichstag, the German "parliament" building, took place on February 27, 1933, less than a month after Hitler took power as Chancellor. It can be likened to the U.S. Capitol burning to the ground. The Nazis accused Marinus van der Lubbe, a Dutch radical, of having set the fire; historians debate whether the Nazis themselves started or had a hand in the fire. In any event, Hitler used the event to eliminate all political opposition. Author K. Hilderand writes:

> The disputed question of who caused the fire…is not of prime importance in this connection: the main point is the use made of it by the Nazis to seize and consolidate power. On the day after the fire, which profoundly shocked the general public, von Hindenburg on the advice of the Cabinet issued a "decree for the protection of the people and state" which in effect abolished the basic political rights conferred by the Weimar constitution, although this remained theoretically in force throughout the twelve years of Nazi rule. The decree created a permanent state of emergency and thus gave a cloak of legality to the persecution and terrorisation of the regime's political opponents.[2]

The lesson that American Conservatives took from the Reichstag fire—that political power can be obtained by convincing the public that one's political opponents are disloyal, even though they are not—is a hallmark of their politics. Conservatives don't just distrust government in a healthy, Locke-ian manner; they view government as an evil. They argue that anyone who seeks to use government to attain useful social purposes, which means

---

1.   Adolph Hitler, *Mein Kampf*, Vol. 1, Ch. 10.
2.   K. Hildebrand, *The Third Reich* (London and New York: Routledge,1984), 4-5.

Liberals, is a socialist, and a socialist is just a communist in sheep's clothing, and therefore an enemy of the United States.

The average person on the street might name former Wisconsin Senator Joseph McCarthy as the worst offender in the Traitor-ism game. At the height of the McCarthy era, a branch of the American Legion labeled the Girl Scouts' "one world" ideas "un-American."[3] When not inspiring his cohorts to denounce the menacing Girl Scouts, McCarthy enjoyed destroying the careers and reputations of those who disagreed that every fifth person was a fifth columnist (and the other four really couldn't be trusted, either). Reports have McCarthy, on his first day as a Senator, calling for striking coal miners to be drafted into the army. Then if they refused to mine they could be court-martialed.[4]

Here's McCarthyism in a nutshell, courtesy of the website history.acusd.edu:

> McCarthy agreed to lead a Republican investigation of communism in the Truman administration. He claimed to have a list of 205 communists in the State Department. Then, he claimed it was 57 names, and then 81. The Senate formed a subcommittee to investigate McCarthy's charges. One of McCarthy's first charges of subversion was against a man named Owen Lattimore, but the subcommittee cleared him within a week. After a few months, Margaret Chase Smith, a Republican Senator from Maine, denounced McCarthy. This did not stop the publication of a list of 151 supposedly subversive entertainers—what Conservatives today call "Hollywood Types." Next, the subcommittee itself denounced McCarthy. McCarthy responded by issuing a long report of his own calling former General and then Secretary of State George Marshall a pawn of a Soviet conspiracy. [Marshall was the genius behind "the Marshall Plan," which was the economic wing of the plan that saved Western Europe from falling to communism.] McCarthy held up President Harry Truman's nomination for ambassador to Russia, and condemned the State Department and the Voice of America. But, McCarthy began to act strangely, including his carrying of a gun. He also began to act like a typical political hack. McCarthy was appointed the head of a minor committee, which he turned into what he hoped would be a semi-permanent body investigating subversion. The main committee lawyer was a man named Roy Cohn. Cohn had a friend

---

3.   *Herblock's History, Political Cartoons from the Crash to the Millenium,* at
     http://lcweb.loc.gov/rr/print/swann/herblock/fire.html

4.   *Spartcus Educational,* at http://www.spartacus.schoolnet.co.uk/
     USAmccarthy.htm

named David Schine, who received a notice he was being drafted. Soon, an army report showed dozens of efforts by McCarthy staff members Roy Cohn and Francis Carr to get preferential treatment for Private Schine. McCarthy began what became known as the "Army-McCarthy" hearings, one of the first big events of the television era, which lasted 36 days. After this lengthy personal exposure, the American public concluded he was a dangerous phony, which gave the Senate the belated courage to censure him. A few years later, McCarthy died from cirrhosis of the liver.[5]

That is quite a record. McCarthy's cirrhosis of the liver was of little or no public import; his cirrhosis of the truth in matters of national security was of great import. Because McCarthy was a liar about matters of national security, even Republicans like Senator "Maggie" Smith of Maine, and eventually the United States Senate as a body, had to denounce him (the vote was 67-22).[6] "McCarthyism" did not become synonymous with a truly over-powerful federal government for nothing. Conservatives, who are so vocally against the federal government doing anything, should have been the loudest squawkers about McCarthy. Instead, Conservatives followed him as their leader, as they had with Mitchell Palmer in the "Red Scare" days of the '20s, and would again with John Mitchell in the "New Left" days of the '60s. Today many still defend Joe McCarthy.

The Conservatives' assault upon Liberals' patriotism is all full of sound and fury, and it's also full of holes, considering that the only ones who served prison terms for subverting the government from within were Conservatives. Certainly, the names "Watergate" and "Iran-Contra" must ring a bell somewhere.

The right wing of fame is filled with people who gained their place in that pantheon by attacking the patriotism of Liberals. The common thread of their rantings unravels even when the ranter is a minor-league villifier like former United States Senator Jesse Helms. Helms once was interviewed by the *Raleigh News & Observer*. Helms, the new Chairman of the Senate Foreign Relations Committee, said former President Clinton was so unpopular on military bases in North Carolina that "he better watch out if he comes down here. He'd better have a bodyguard."[7]

---

5.   "Joseph McCarthy," at http://history.acusd.edu/gen/20th/1950s/
     mccarthy.html
6.   Jesse Friedman, "The Fight For America: Senator Joseph McCarthy,"
     5th Revision, 3rd Edit, at http://www.mccarthy.cjb.net/

The "unpatriotic" accusation by Conservatives takes many forms, but the theme is consistent. Paul Begala observes:

> Richard Nixon got elected to the Senate by calling his Democratic opponent, Helen Gahagan Douglas, "pink right down to her underwear." George H. W. Bush attacked Michael Dukakis's patriotism throughout the 1988 presidential-election campaign. Rich Bond, former chairman of the Republican National Committee, once said that Democrats were not "real Americans." And we all remember the elder Bush darkly hinting that Bill Clinton's student-backpacking trip to Moscow in the 1960s somehow made his patriotism suspect.
>
> But in the wake of the September 11 terrorist attacks against the United States, it is enlightening to examine who has been patriotic and who has been partisan. Though there have been plenty of policy disagreements, the Democrats have stood behind their commander in chief, whatever their doubts about his fitness for office or how he attained it. Senate majority leader Tom Daschle and House minority leader Dick Gephardt issued statements of unwavering solidarity. Former President Bill Clinton called on all Americans to rally behind George W. Bush. In a rare public statement, Al Gore put patriotism ahead of the fact that a majority of Americans had wanted him to be president—and he bear-hugged Bush. Even a hard-core partisan like Terry McAuliffe, chairman of the Democratic National Committee, ordered a cease-fire, going so far as to remove any criticism of Bush from the party's Web site....
>
> In the days after hate-filled fanatics murdered thousands of innocent people on American soil, the Reverend Jerry Falwell described those cowards as instruments of God's divine retribution. Appearing on the 700 Club (hosted by the Reverend Pat Robertson), Falwell uttered this gem about the mass slaughter: "God continues to lift the curtain and allow the enemies of America to give us probably what we deserve." He went on to say that the American Civil Liberties Union has "got to take a lot of blame for this," then added to his indictment judges and others who are "throwing God out of the public square." Then Falwell got specific. "The abortionists have got to bear some burden for this because God will not be mocked," he said. "And when we destroy 40 million little innocent babies, we make God mad. I really believe that the pagans, and the abortionists, and the feminists, and the gays and the lesbians who are actively trying to make that an alternative lifestyle, the ACLU, People for the American Way—all of them

---

7. "The Columbia World of Quotations," 1996, *Bartleby.com*, at http://www.bartleby.com/66/41/27741.html

who have tried to secularize America—I point the finger in their face and say, 'You helped this happen.'"[8]

Attacking opponents' patriotism is an old Conservative trick and was one of the major motivations for the Nixon gang's criminal conspiracy to subvert this country's Constitution, which rightfully drove Nixon from office. Watergate historian Keith Olson reports:

> Considering critics as traitors or enemies and therefore as a threat to the nation was hardly new in February, 1972. In March, 1971 [Pat] Buchanan had looked ahead to the 1972 campaign and written, "If the President goes, we all go, and maybe the country with us." A further example of this White House mindset was the "enemies list" John Dean compiled in 1971 and to which [Charles] Colson, Buchanan, and others contributed. The list, which grew to more than 200, included movie stars such as Paul Newman, the professional football player Joe Namath, and college presidents, along with the expected newspaper and television figures, including Daniel Schorr of CBS. Democratic senators Kennedy, Muskie, and Mondale also made the list. Nixon aides' portrayal of opponents and critics as enemies seemed to rationalize breaking the law. In an election year, both the mindset and the rationalization for illegal activity intensified; after all, enemies were a threat to the nation.[9]

Part of the Nixon conspiracy was to place Donald Segretti in charge of a secret program to disrupt the Democratic primaries through a series of "dirty tricks."[10] Never mind that these dirty tricks essentially disenfranchised Democratic primary voters by feeding them false information. After all, Conservatives had been disenfranchising African-Americans in the South for generations, so they were good at it. For instance, Olson continues:

> One of Segretti's infiltrators stole Muskie campaign stationery and mailed a fraudulent letter to 300 supporters of fellow contenders in the Democratic primary, Senator Henry Jackson of Washington State and Hubert Humphrey of Minnesota. The letter sought to make its readers "aware of several

---

8.   Paul Begala, "Sunshine Patriots," *Lehigh County Democratic Committee of Pennsylvania*, October 18, 2001, at http://www.lehighdems.org/011018begala.html

9.   Keith W. Olson, *Watergate, The Presidential Scandal That Shook America* (University of Kansas Press, 2003), 30.

10. *Ibid.*, 30.

facts," among them that Jackson had fathered a child with an unmarried teenager, that twice police had arrested him on homosexual charges, and that police had arrested Humphrey, while in the company of a prostitute, for driving under the influence of alcohol.[11]

Maybe Segretti merely made a series of innocent mistakes. Perhaps he mixed-up Senator Jackson with Senator Thurmond as far as the "child with teenage mother" matter or (other than the arrests) with J. Edgar Hoover or Roy Cohn in the homosexual matter. Possibly he confused (except for the prostitute part) Senator Humphrey with George W. Bush or Dick Cheney as far as the DUI arrests. [12]

Evidently carrying forward with the general Conservative viewpoint that political opponents are the agents of enemy nations, "the Nixon campaign placed a great emphasis on intelligence gathering.... The most important intelligence operation in terms of its impact stemmed from a plan of Gordon Liddy."[13] As they discussed Liddy's plan, Nixon aides identified three main areas at risk—Lawrence F. O'Brien's Watergate office; O'Brien's hotel suite during the Democratic convention; and the eventual Democratic presidential nominee's headquarters.[14] But Nixon in particular, and Conservatives in general, missed and continue to miss the point. Writes historian Fred Emery: "The duty is clear on the part of elected government to act to protect life, ensure domestic tranquility, and guard national security. But in resorting to methods beyond the law, the Nixon men fell into a classic trap: They failed to distinguish between what would be broadly accepted in a democracy as necessity in pursuit of the common good and what would be abhorrent as abuse when perverted for party interest."[15]

The Watergate fiasco serves as a fine example of the logical consequence of the Conservative view that Liberals are this country's enemies. As chronicled by the website people.memphis.edu, on June 13 The *New York Times*

11. *Ibid.*, 31.
12. "Segretti testifies about 'dirty tricks,'" *MSNBC*, October 3, 1973, at http://www.msnbc.com/onair/msnbc/timeandagain/archive/watergate/oct373.asp
13. Olson, 36-37.
14. *Ibid.*, 37.
15. Fred Emery, *Watergate* (New York: Times Books, a division of Random House, 1994), 25.

began to print the Pentagon Papers, which had been commissioned by
Robert McNamara and supplied to the newspaper by Daniel Ellsberg, who
had worked on them while changing from a Vietnam War supporter to
opponent. Nixon's attempts through the legal process to stop their publication failed when the Supreme Court did not prevent the newspaper from
going forward. Nixon did not accept this defeat. Instead, he commissioned
a private intelligence group to burglarize Ellsberg's office in the hope of
finding something with which to discredit him. Liddy then presented a
broader plan, which besides the break-ins already mentioned, also included
wiretapping, sabotage, kidnapping, mugging squads and the use of prosti-
tutes for political blackmail. This group was called the "Plumbers," and
they pulled off some successful break-ins before being caught at the Watergate building. Nixon, in conjunction with John Mitchell, then the Attorney
General of the United States, and his chief staff members, John Erlichmann and Robert Haldeman, proceeded to hatch a plot to cover-up
everything and deny any White House involvement.

The United States Senate opened an investigation, during which it stum-
bled upon the fact that Nixon had taped a great number of White House
meetings, including some that outlined most of the plot. Other events—one
of the Plumber's wives died in a plane crash with $100,000 in "hush money" in
her possession, for example—further broke open the scandal. Eventually,
Mitchell, Haldeman, Erlichman, the Plumbers (including Liddy), and many
others went to prison for their roles in the illegal conspiracy to deprive Americans of their Constitutional rights and the cover-up of the illegal activity. The
U.S. House of Representatives voted Articles of Impeachment against Nixon,
and in the face of an inevitable conviction in the Senate, he resigned from the
presidency. While the investigation was being completed, the country also
enjoyed the spectacle of Nixon's Vice-President, Spiro Agnew, pleading "no
contest" to charges he took bribes from highway contractors while governor of
Maryland—a sort of personal "Social Security" plan—and his resignation pre-
ceded Nixon's.[16]

As her insidious new book, *Treason, Liberal Treachery From The Cold War
To The War On Terrorism* shows, Anne Coulter out-McCarthys McCarthy and
out-Nixons Nixon. It is strange that Coulter writes books, because her intellectual mentor, McCarthy, so disdained them and wasted taxpayer dollars
identifying "anti-American" books.[17]

---

16. "Watergate Chronology," at http://www.people.memphis.edu/
    ~sherman/chronoWatergate.htm

The first chapter of Coulter's book, entitled "Fifty Years of Treason," opens with her thesis:

"Liberals have a preternatural gift for striking a position on the side of treason."[18] She continues, "Everyone says liberals love America, too. No they don't. Whenever the nation is under attack, from within or without, liberals side with the enemy. This is their essence."[19] Oddly, Coulter equates Liberals with Democrats, Democrats with Socialists, and Socialists with Communists, but never explains how it is that our closest ally in the War on Terror and the Iraq War is Great Britain, run by Tony Blair, a member of the English Labor Party.

In everyday hyperbole among friends or family, people make all sorts of wild charges against politicians that are meant not to be taken literally, but rather to make a point by exaggerating truth. However, using the words "traitor" or "treason" to describe an opponent's status or actions is a fish of a different fin, because to accuse someone of that is to accuse the person of a crime, and a capital one at that. Under the law, such an accusation is defamatory *per se*, which means that general damages are awarded automatically, even if no particular damages are proved, because the law assumes damages flowing from the mere accusation. Defamation is not covered by the normal free speech protections of the First Amendment, and can give rise to lawsuits. The reason that an accusation of treason is automatically assumed to harm the target is the very reason Coulter used it: the accusation inflames passions.

When one is truly guilty of treason, and has therefore un-pledged his or her allegiance to the flag, there comes into being an adversarial relationship between the nation and the former citizen whose loyalty was previously mandated. Coulter may think that she is clever or merely tweaking the nose of Liberals by calling them treasonous, but she is neither. If Liberals are treasonous, then the bonds between them and the United States are shattered, and the situation justifies a clash of arms between them. That means a new Civil War. I don't think Coulter has the courage for the country to follow through on her logic, or perhaps she does not understand it. Since our only Civil War occurred when the Conservative traitors—*actual* traitors who put on the gray uniform to become our modern Conservatives' icons of "cultural heri-

---

17. *Spartacus Educational*, at http://www.spartacus.schoolnet.co.uk/
    USAmccarthy.htm
18. Coulter, *Treason*, 1
19. *Ibid.*, 1.

tage"—shot at Old Glory and the men carrying it, Coulter's "preternatural ability" to put Americans at each other's throats is all the more wicked and in contravention of her alleged intellect.

It would be unfair to say that Coulter falls into the Conservative trap of "us versus them," because she is the one setting that trap for those of her fellow citizens gullible enough to believe she has something of merit to communicate. The "us versus them" way of looking at the world is self-defeating in almost every way. When the South seceded from the North, it was crushed. When Teddy Roosevelt split the Republican party, both it and the splinter Bull Moosers were crushed. When Goldwater ran to purify the Republican party as one for Conservatives only, he was crushed. When McGovern ran to make the Democratic party safe only for the then Politically Correct crowd, he was crushed. But when Reagan ran under a "big tent," he won. When Clinton ran to the center, he won.

We can run our country as people all dedicated to the proposition—and to each other even when we disagree—or we can run it to maintain a particular group's concepts of purity. Coulter does not consider, or did consider and unwisely rejected, the notion that when our troops are in harm's way, the biggest thing that ought to separate them is whether they like the Lakers or the Knicks. They should respect each other's politics. Fox TV's Bill O'Reilly does not agree with Liberals, but he generally shows them and their views respect. Coulter, conversely, actually incites violence of "her type" of Americans against Liberals when she writes:

> Instead of wondering why foreigners hate Americans, a more fruitful inquiry for the Democrats might be to ask why *Americans* are beginning to hate Democrats [emphasis added].[20]

There you have it: Conservatives' two-part "philosophy." They, first, believe that *they* are the true Americans while Liberals are not and, second, advocate that true Americans should *hate* non-Americans. Conservatives have hated and continue to hate African-Americans, "immigrants," poor people, working people (especially, but not only, those who like unions), and now "Democrats," which means, in their definition, anybody who is a Liberal. Not

---

20. *Ibid.*, 230. Of course, if Coulter had her wish, and the Red States did take on the Blue States in a replay of 1861-1865, the outcome would be the same.

all Conservatives are haters; many identify with Conservatism mainly because of its "limited government" arguments. But high-profile Conservatives like Coulter whip up hatred, and some of them, including Coulter, no longer even try to disguise it. They transform the buzz words "States' Rights," "local control," "federalism" (as of late), and "limited government" into hate words because, in the particular context of this nation's history, these words have been hijacked by the haters.

It is not even amusing that the only people ever prosecuted wrongly, in Coulter's opinion, are Conservatives who have tried to subvert the Constitution that she and other Conservatives maintain is the center of their concern. Coulter spends page after page of her latest "book" defending Joe McCarthy, censored by his fellow Senators.[21] Then she says that "Watergate would be the left's ultimate revenge against him for telling the truth about Hiss."[22] The "Left" may have been thinking a lot of things about Watergate, but I guarantee that getting revenge for Alger Hiss was low on the list.[23]

Ollie North of Iran-Contra infamy and her other TV friends were not really guilty of anything, according to Coulter, because they were merely indicted on charges of taking action "[t]hat was intended, among other things, to support military and paramilitary operations in Nicaragua by the Contras and to conduct covert action operations. Democrats thought it should be a criminal offense to give aid to anti-Communists."[24] No, Ms. Coulter, Liberals believe that foreign policy should be constituted by the legitimate authorities of the United States, so if some Liberal is trading with Castro today in violation of the sanctions against him, we should go ahead and put the Liberal in jail—but not for advocating the lifting of sanctions. Coulter admits that the Iran-Contra conspirators engaged in their misdeeds even though those actions were not approved by President Ronald Reagan![25] In Coulter's world, the farther right your politics, the more right are your actions, the law notwithstand-

---

21. *Ibid.*
22. *Ibid.*, 10.
23. Probably, .00000001% of the population supported Nixon's impeachment because of the Alger Hiss matter. That figure is obtained by dividing the approximate population of the United States—200,000,000—in 1974 by the number of then sons of Julius and Ethel Rosenberg—2.
24. Coulter, *Treason*, 178.
25. *Ibid.*, 178.

ing. All that "Constitutional" stuff really is just window-dressing for the secret paramilitary organizations she believes should be running America.

At the same time, Coulter's view that all Liberals are traitors actually weakens our military, because it tends to make our soldiers—some of whom are Conservative, some of whom are Liberal, and some of whom are in the middle somewhere—distrust each other. Coulter's charge is not only wrong and defamatory; it is just plain senseless and contrary to national security, because if it were taken seriously, it would denigrate the military's unit cohesion.

This is the nub of the issue—traitors and foxholes. Coulter, the Conservatives' Grand Representative, has called all Liberals on active duty traitors—whether in the United States, Iraq, or Afghanistan. This vituperative vixen must think, assuming she does think, that Liberals are not serving in our military. As bartcop.com, a website that gives the military service of many politicians and other prominent people, discloses, this smearing as "unpatriotic" of Liberal politicians who have served their country in uniform is all too common from Conservatives who have not. While lack of military service is not any indication at all of lack of patriotism, nevertheless Liberals who did serve include Gray Davis, George McGovern, Richard Gephardt, Tom Daschle, Al Gore, Charles Rangel, Ted Kennedy, John Kerry, and Max Cleland, while Conservatives Dick Armey, Bill Bennett, Dick Cheney, Tom DeLay, Newt Gingrich, Phil Gramm, Rush Limbaugh, Trent Lott, Ken Starr, Karl Rove, and John Ashcroft never did.[26] Yet, Conservatives un-loyally assert all the former are traitors, and all the latter are patriots.

Perhaps all of these Conservatives could not serve or fight because patriotic African-Americans so flooded the enlistment offices that there just wasn't room for anyone else. This laughable explanation was actually offered by Representative Tom "the Exterminator" DeLay of Texas, the leader of *all* the Republicans in the United States House of Representatives. Tim Fleck writes in the *Houston Press*:

> In 1988, a little-known Texas congressman gathered a crowd of reporters in the lobby of a downtown New Orleans hotel housing several state delegates to the Republican National Convention. Clutching a pole topped by a drooping American flag, 22nd District two-termer Tom DeLay launched

---

26. "Military records of our leaders," *Bartcop.com*, at
   http://www.bartcop.com/warvets.htm

into a rather implausible defense of Dan Quayle, an Indiana senator freshly picked by George Bush as his presidential ticket partner.

Bill Clinton's draft-dodging efforts would become an issue in his successful campaign against Bush four years later, but now Quayle's own past manipulation of family ties to get into a national guard unit was touching off a classic feeding frenzy among the convention press corps.

DeLay seemed to feel the issue applied personally to him, and perhaps it did. He had graduated from the University of Houston at the height of the Vietnam conflict in 1970, but chose to enlist in the war on cockroaches, fleas and termites as the owner of an exterminator business, rather than going off to battle against the Vietcong.

He and Quayle, DeLay explained to the assembled media in New Orleans, were victims of an unusual phenomenon back in the days of the undeclared Southeast Asian war. So many minority youths had volunteered for the well-paying military positions to escape poverty and the ghetto that there was literally no room for patriotic folks like himself. Satisfied with the pronouncement, which dumbfounded more than a few of his listeners who had lived the sixties, DeLay marched off to the convention.[27]

That should restore everybody's lost faith in the Conservative establishment. In contrast, a McGovern biographer writes:

George McGovern was the Democratic candidate for President in 1972. McGovern was at 22 a decorated Army Air Force pilot who had flown 35 combat missions (the maximum number allowed), who, with two of his plane's four engines knocked out, somehow managed through skill and strength an emergency landing of his B-24 (which required a 5,000 foot landing strip) on a 2,200 foot runway on an island in the Adriatic.[28]

---

27. Tim Fleck, "Which Bug Gets the Gas? Will the next house DeLay fumigates be that big White one or his own?" *Houston Press*, January 7, 1999, at http://houstonpress.com/issues/1999-01-07/columns2.html/1/index.html

28. Mark Shields, "Stephen Ambrose Brings Us George McGovern, War Hero," *Seattle Post-Intelligencer*, September 10, 2001, republished by *Common Dreams News Center*, at http://www.commondreams.org/views01/0910-04.htm

McGovern's heroism did not stop Coulter from calling him a communist, under the theory that a fourth-party candidate in 1948, former Vice President of the United States Henry A. Wallace, ran a "Communist-dominated" and "Soviet-backed" presidential campaign, which McGovern praised and compared to his own 1972 campaign.[29]

The Conservatives' sorry crowding into the last refuge of scoundrels reached its saddest nadir in the 2002 campaign for a United States Senate Seat in Georgia. In that race, incumbent Max Cleland, a United States Senator from Georgia who in Vietnam lost three of his limbs for all of us, was unsuccessful in retaining his seat. In large part Cleland lost because he said such unwise things as, "We need to make sure that we look after our workers. More and more of our workers are being laid off and this economy is taking a dive," rather than reflexively voting in favor of the Bush Administration's version of a Department of Homeland Security, which took away certain important civil service rights of government employees.[30] This caused Cleland's opponent, now Senator Saxby Chambliss, to mount a vicious attack on Cleland's patriotism. Chambliss aired a television ad wherein, according to *USA Today*:

> Images of both bin Laden and Saddam are on the screen in a TV ad that Georgia Republican Rep. Saxby Chambliss began airing Friday in his bid to unseat Democratic Sen. Max Cleland. The ad attacks Cleland as weak and "misleading" on homeland security.[31]

Despite Cleland's military service, Chambliss even attacked Cleland for "failing to defend the country."[32] Thus, does the "big lie" work even in America.

Perhaps a future Liberal President is currently serving in Iraq or Afghanistan. That will not stop Conservatives from attacking his or her patriotism because it is not only Coulter, personally, who holds such vile views. Rather, it

---

29. Coulter, *Treason*, 193.
30. "Cleland Lead Shrinks in Georgia Senate Race," *Fox News*, October 22, 2002, at http://www.foxnews.com/story/0,2933,66293,00.html
31. William M. Welch, "Republicans using Iraq issue to slam election opponents," *USA Today*, October 13, 2002, at http://www.usatoday.com/news/washington/2002-10-13-iraq-politics_x.htm
32. S. Heather Duncan, "Chambliss, Cleland slugging it out," *The Telegraph*, November 1, 2002, at http://www.macon.com/mld/telegraph/4417097.htm

is endemic to Conservatives in general. For instance, in the 2000 Presidential recount in Florida, Conservative Governor Marc Raciot, now President Bush's campaign manager, said about candidate Al Gore: "Last night we learned how far the vice president's campaign will go to win this election. And I am very sorry to say but the vice president's lawyers have gone to war, in my judgment, against the men and women who serve in our armed forces."[33] Conservatives just don't understand that the military comprises people holding a wide range of political views and fights for us all. This means that true support for the military requires supporting its Liberals, Conservatives, and Moderates, not just the soldiers of whose politics Conservatives approve.[34]

I'll also bet that the 24,000 veterans who marched in Washington on April 23, 1971, "and threw their medals over a fence that kept them away from the Capitol" as a protest against the Vietnam War, know a whole lot more about patriotism than Coulter does.[35]

---

33. "Schwarzkopf, Others Criticize Rejection of Military Votes," *The Star News*, November 19, 2000, at http://www.shelbystar.com/news2000/_disc4/00000b0c.htm

34. In *Treason*, Coulter makes no mention, in her many pages of praise for McCarthy, whether McCarthy's main investigative lawyer, Roy Cohn, or J. Edgar Hoover, favored gay marriage.

35. *Watergate, The Presidential Scandal That Shook America*, by Keith W. Olson, University of Kansas Press (2003) at 29.

Reason 6. Liberals Support an Active Foreign Policy Within Constitutional Limits.

Our Revolutionary Principles

The United States of America was born of a revolution designed to promote worldwide liberal, democratic, capitalistic, Constitutional government through the creation of a nation state whose purpose was to foster an environment conducive to the creation of other such nation states. In order to be true to our birthright, our foreign policy should therefore always be guided by two goals: the protection of the exercise of American freedom at home and the promotion of American principles abroad.

The first goal was established in the Preamble to the United States Constitution, in which the People state that they have formed the Union in order to, among other things, provide for the common defense. The second goal was specified in the Declaration of Independence, which states that all people are born with certain inalienable rights, and that governments that trample on those rights may be abolished or altered. Inalienable rights are those that cannot be given away even with the consent of those who possess them. Our national philosophy is that people are born free, and they have no right to become un-free.

Our philosophy rejects the premise that the world is divided between rich and poor nations, industrial and underdeveloped nations, northern and southern nations, or any other artificial division. We should therefore reject any conclusions that follow in the wake of such distinctions—conclusions that might, for example, have us siding with the underdeveloped against the developed or vice versa.

Our country should instead enjoy the most cordial relations with those nations that can best help us continue to enjoy our lives under our own Constitutional form and freedoms because they understand and share our core values. Only America's friends fit this first category. Our next level of friendly relations are for allies. When the issue is the protection of our own country, it does not matter whether the ally is free or unfree, as demonstrated by the need to ally with a Stalin to defeat a Hitler. However, this does not mean that the conduct of our friends and allies should not bear heavily upon our consciences, because it is our duty to promote inalienable rights everywhere.

None of this means that we should be unrealistic Wilsonian idealists who believe that we can transport our democratic system to every nation on the globe—though we should keep that ideal in mind—or that the United States has an unrestricted right to interfere with other countries' internal affairs, or that it should want to interfere even if it did have such a right. Each nation must adapt for itself the basic love of freedom with its own traditions and needs. A cornerstone of American foreign policy is tolerance for the rights and beliefs of other nations.

On the other hand, tolerance has limits. Just as America must offer equitable solutions, equitably arrived at, America also has the duty, where possible, to promote equitable solutions through strength only. America should not stand by idly and allow evil things to happen just because we are tolerant. As the English, French and Italians can testify, freedom must sometimes be won and, as the Germans and Japanese can testify, sometimes it must be imposed by force of arms.

On the most practical level, the United States must be guided by its own self-interest. Our self-interest can be mere power relationships or economic interests upon occasion. Because our nation is dedicated to a proposition, however, our true and fundamental interest is usually Lincoln's proposition, not the mere power relationship or economic interest. American leaders must above all serve our country and our revolution.

Lessons From The Twentieth Century

Last century was marked by the false and evil revolutions of Marx/Lenin/Stalin on the left and Hitler on the right. These revolutions, often mixing their genes with existing cultures, had many children, including Mao, Castro,

Ortega, Mussolini, Franco, Pinochet, Mugabe, Hirohito, Pol Pot, Khomeini, Nasser, Kaddafi, and Saddam Hussein. In a perverse way, these leaders underscore the common delusions of all humanity, and therefore ironically give some hope for common solutions. These abhorrent parents and their bastard children sometimes attempted to steal our birthright as the world's only true revolutionaries. Our country has from time to time found itself in all sorts of trouble with these false revolutionaries because our country—on the whole at least aspiring to be a peaceful, civilized, tolerant, and free people—often has made the mistake of believing that these others had the same aspirations.

Marxism is—perhaps *was*—heaven's way of testing human gullibility. Marxism calls itself "scientific" socialism. By this, the Marxists mean to tell us they have studied all evidence of the social fabric and have come to the one, true conclusion regarding its organization. Marxists do not believe they are influenced by the "utopian" dreams of their socialist forebears and contemporaries. Marxists believe that they have coldly seen the "whole picture" of world history.

Of course, Marx did not see the whole picture at all. He saw only the most minute beginning of the modern world's only true revolution, the "bourgeois" capitalist revolution. The bourgeois revolution is our revolution, the French revolution without the terror, and is dynamic to its core. The other revolutions are coups that change governments and power relationships stemming from the coups. The bourgeois revolution builds and rebuilds society at a startling pace, but attempts to keep the evolving rules of the social contract fair in the meantime (though it sometimes loses or surrenders to oligarchy or monopoly on the capitalist side and totalitarianism on the other). Our forebears lived through the industrial revolution. Most of us have lived to see the computer revolution transform our society, but it will not be long before, mid-mouse-click, capitalism will generate another revolution that will mystify and confuse us.

In 1917, an unfortunate event occurred. The then rare but powerful virus of Marxism ravaged the already sick and deranged personalities of two common criminals, Lenin and Stalin. Lunacy married murder, and the world, logically and naturally, was therefore left to contend with lunatic murderers. Then, in Germany, the bourgeois revolution backtracked. It embraced Prussianism, Leninist single-partyism, and simple hatred, and made industrial technology do its bidding. Our own international revolution was left to face communist and Nazi holocausts.

German-American Bund members and isolationists like Charles Lind-bergh wanted us to either surrender, condone, or copy fascism, which prom-ised a new mold for mankind. Meanwhile, the American far-left, and some not so far, wanted to be part of building a Soviet-styled "new man." This led a few, like Julius and Ethel Rosenberg, to commit espionage (meaning *actual* treason), and others—unlike them, well-meaning—such as Alger Hiss, to at least approach it.

The false revolutionaries of the left and the right thought our revolution was inefficient, outmoded, and doomed to failure. In reality, it was their mur-derous revolutions that represented doom, and our revolution correctly identi-fied those enemies and largely defeated them, although China looms as a huge open question. We debated containment and counterinsurgency, but our mid-dle held—first because we *are* the middle, and second because our capitalist military industrial complex, both the necessary and corrupt parts, is a superior form of organization and at least turned out enough tanks, planes, and ships to give us the opportunity to criticize that complex while facing the enemy. There is a qualitative difference between Stalin's enemies list, which had everyone's name on it and quite a different reward for appearing on it, and Nixon's. It is because of our low tolerance for such things that we inoculated ourselves against those such as Stalin's by taking a dose of Nixon's.

No, the common mentor of Marxism and Nazism is death. Death by star-vation as a government policy. Death by race-killing as a government policy. Death, Death, Death. Brutal, cruel, nihilistic, and sadistic Death. Such Death is the implacable enemy of our revolution. Death driven by believers who would say and do anything to accomplish their deadly goals. Stormtrooper guards, concentration camp guards, gulag guards, Khmer Rouge guards, Red Guards. The "new men" served as agents of these philosophies of death and motivated whole elites, sometimes whole peoples, to lie, cheat, steal, rape, plunder, burn, and murder their way across most of this planet. Tens, thou-sands, hundreds of thousands, millions, and finally tens of millions of people were killed, more tens of millions were wounded, and billions suffered on account of these false revolutions of hate.

By 1945, we had learned that if it looks like a mass murderer, it is, and that it is necessary to kill the mass murderer before the murderer kills you. Although average Americans just wanted to work at their jobs, go to the play or the ballgame, and relax with their families, and although apologists wrote many books that argued against opposing this "agrarian reformer" or that "nationalist," the barbed wire and crematoria demonstrated once and for all why the Liberal foreign policy as eventually institutionalized by Franklin Roosevelt had to carry the day.

Liberal Internationalism Requires Constitutionalism

It was the Liberal Abraham Lincoln who waged war to free the slaves; it was the Liberal Woodrow Wilson who took on the Kaiser to make the world safe for democracy; it was the Liberal Franklin Roosevelt who defeated the mass murderers Hitler, Tojo, and Mussolini to make the world safe for human life itself, and it was the Liberal Harry Truman who took on the North Koreans and the Chinese to stem the tide of tyranny's advance. These were all Liberal wars that caused the United States to become more liberal by making us face up to our responsibilities as world citizens.

Conversely, isolationism has been the traditional Conservative position in this country, because it goes hand in hand with keeping local tyrannies in power. From Charles Lindbergh to Father Coughlin to Robert Taft, it was those who were in favor of limited government at home who had the greatest fear of an active role for the United States in the world because an active role in the world necessitated a strong federal government, and a strong federal government was a threat to States' Rights. There is still a segment of this isolationist Conservative movement afoot in the United States. Though a supporter of late of George W. Bush's wars, Pat Buchanan claimed that the first Gulf War was fomented by Israel's "amen corner" and has generally advocated staying home. Even Bush himself was not immune to the traditional isolationism. In the Second Presidential Debate of 2000, he belittled President Clinton's "nation-building," which was in the great Liberal tradition. In that debate, Bush stated:

> Somalia started off as a humanitarian mission and then changed into a nation-building mission, and that's where the mission went wrong. The mission was changed and, as a result, our nation paid a price. And so I don't think our troops ought to be used for what's called nation-building. I think our troops ought to be used to fight and win war. I think our troops ought to be used to help overthrow a dictator that's in our—when it's in our best interests. But in this case, it was a nation-building exercise. And the same with Haiti, I wouldn't have supported, either.... I don't think so. I think what we need to do is convince people who live in the lands they live in to build the nations. Maybe I'm missing something here. I mean, we're going to have kind of a nation-building corps from America? Absolutely

not. Our military is meant to fight and win war; that's what it's meant to do. And when it gets overextended, morale drops.[1]

Subsequent events on 9/11 eventually won over George W. Bush, but Buchanan is still uneasy about our Iraq venture, because he is uncertain whether he favors Israeli democracy over Arab dictatorships. Of course, the even more extreme right is extremely isolationist. The Timothy McVeighs of the country regard an internationalist foreign policy as a ruse to bring foreign rule to this country, which will be capped by black UN helicopters dropping in troops that will want to enslave all the white Anglo-Saxons of the country in favor of some "race-mongrelizing" dictator.

Somehow, Liberals have allowed the right wing to steal our foreign policy, which normally fosters engagement in the world, because of fears of repeating our experience in Vietnam. Obviously, that conflict did pose serious questions for our Liberal principles, but many of us unfortunately threw out the baby with the bath water. We are not wrong to advocate multilateralism and, some-times, intervention. What happened in Vietnam was that all the Presidents who conducted that war refused to use the proper procedures as laid out in the Constitution. This failure exponentially multiplied the force of the political and military defeat we suffered there, and so traumatized many Liberals. Now, even if the proper procedures were used, many Liberals would still refuse to engage the world.

Conservatives have been reluctantly won over to our former position little by little, just as Liberals abandoned it. Therefore, foreign policy might present a unique opportunity for the great majority of Americans to find common ground. The problem is that the purpose of a (political) opposition is to oppose. Foreign policy has been conducted in the realm of our national repre-sentatives taking positions that show personal loyalty or opposition to the offi-cial in the White House and appeal to patriotism at its most simple, rather than conducting a level-headed discussion of what makes sense for America.

This muddled state of affairs can be corrected only if Liberals and Conser-vatives first agree on the purposes of our foreign policy, and then apply the procedures already contained in our Constitution to carry out those purposes. This will effectuate a foreign policy that calls for America to be a good world

---

1.   "The 2nd Presidential Debate," *PBS Online*, October 11, 2000, at http: //www.pbs.org/newshour/bb/election/2000debates/2ndebate2.html

citizen—proactive when necessary, but nonetheless subject to all the restraints of our Constitution.

Ironically, George W. Bush has been following a Liberal foreign policy, despite his campaign's semi-isolationism that rejected nation-building and called the Somalia and Kosovo campaigns foolish at heart.[2] Bush's problem has been that he has followed that policy in some important respects badly, in that while he has properly attacked the mass murderers, he has offended many of our allies in the process and has failed to win over the hearts and minds of many fence-sitters. On the whole, it is marginally better for Bush to run a Liberal foreign policy poorly than a Conservative foreign policy expertly, but this is quite a waste when it is altogether possible to have the Liberal foreign policy run well. The cause of this dichotomy, of course, is that Bush is running a foreign policy that is at odds with the Conservative view that America should isolate itself from the world, while a truly Liberal foreign policy would try to convince the world to come over to our way of thinking.

Immediately after 9/11, Bush received praise from Liberals and Conservatives alike because he quickly detailed our principles and called for the rest of the world to stand with us. At that time, Bush correctly set the tone by saying that, like other countries, America was a citizen of the world and, as it had been wrongfully attacked, needed the assistance of other nations. In those days, Bush's words spoke of the American melting pot where a person's heritage is not his or her yoke—a country that is kind to strangers. Indeed, to the external world, Bush used the words one would expect from a Liberal on the domestic stump. For instance, on September 20, 2001, in his address to a Joint Session of Congress, Bush said:

> We have seen the state of our Union in the endurance of rescuers, working past exhaustion. We have seen the unfurling of flags, the lighting of candles, the giving of blood, the saying of prayers—in English, Hebrew, and Arabic. We have seen the decency of a loving and giving people who have made the grief of strangers their own.

---

2.   The Conservative criticism of the Somalia campaign because of the horrible loss of the "Blackhawk Down" Rangers has always been particularly puzzling. The Somalia venture was an overwhelming success. The United States went to Somalia to stop the starvation, not to destroy an enemy army or conquer territory. We accomplished our goal. As in most every war, there were casualties that could or should have been avoided.

Bush's words had impact because they spoke of unity while at the same time recognizing the country's diversity. Next, he integrated America into the world community and acknowledged that even we need the world's help to solve our problems:

> And on behalf of the American people, I thank the world for its outpouring of support. America will never forget the sounds of our National Anthem playing at Buckingham Palace, on the streets of Paris, and at Berlin's Brandenburg Gate.
>
> We will not forget South Korean children gathering to pray outside our embassy in Seoul, or the prayers of sympathy offered at a mosque in Cairo. We will not forget moments of silence and days of mourning in Australia and Africa and Latin America.
>
> ...This is not, however, just America's fight. And what is at stake is not just America's freedom. This is the world's fight. This is civilization's fight. This is the fight of all who believe in progress and pluralism, tolerance and freedom.
>
> We ask every nation to join us. We will ask, and we will need, the help of police forces, intelligence services, and banking systems around the world. The United States is grateful that many nations and many international organizations have already responded—with sympathy and with support. Nations from Latin America, to Asia, to Africa, to Europe, to the Islamic world. Perhaps the NATO Charter reflects best the attitude of the world: An attack on one is an attack on all.

Bush continued on such themes by talking against hate, concentrating instead on what we all have in common:

> I ask you to uphold the values of America, and remember why so many have come here. We are in a fight for our principles, and our first responsibility is to live by them. No one should be singled out for unfair treatment or unkind words because of their ethnic background or religious faith.

Neither did Bush forget that even in the face of our own losses at the hands of murderers, we could not lose sight of our goal to advance human freedom:

> Great harm has been done to us. We have suffered great loss. And in our grief and anger we have found our mission and our moment. Freedom and fear are at war. The advance of human freedom—the great achievement of

our time, and the great hope of every time—now depends on us. Our nation—this generation—will lift a dark threat of violence from our people and our future. We will rally the world to this cause by our efforts, by our courage. We will not tire, we will not falter, and we will not fail.[3]

Bush continued these Liberal themes when he addressed the United Nations General Assembly on November 10, 2001. Bush noted that:

If we were to read the names of every person who died [on 9/11], it would take more than three hours. Those names include a citizen of Gambia, whose wife spent their fourth wedding anniversary, September the 12th, searching in vain for her husband. Those names include a man who supported his wife in Mexico, sending home money every week. Those names include a young Pakistani who prayed toward Mecca five times a day and died that day trying to save others.

What Bush did not do on this historic occasion was refer to rugged individualism, characterize the government as the enemy, or admire the "heritage" of the Confederate flag. No, Bush talked instead about Gambians and Pakistanis, and it did not matter that the Mexican he mentioned as sending home money to his wife might not be a documented alien, nor that he was taking money out of the American economy and putting it in Mexico's. There was no talk about people losing their freedom when helped by government—even a foreign one (ours). How unlike it was, though, to the historic Conservative responses to our own problems, foreign and domestic!

Bush even justified the military action that he had put in motion in Afghanistan by highlighting the advancement of women's rights and our *government's* provision of food and other assistance there:

History will record our response and judge or justify every nation in this hall. The civilized world is now responding. We act to defend ourselves and deliver our children from a future of fear. We choose the dignity of life over a culture of death. We choose lawful change and civil disagreement over coercion, subversion and chaos....

---

3. "Address to a Joint Session of Congress and the American People," *The White House* website, September 20, 2001, at http://www. whitehouse.gov/news/releases/2001/09/20010920_8.html

America has airdropped over 1.3 million packages of rations into Afghanistan. Just this week, we airlifted 20,000 blankets and over 200 tons of provisions into the region....

As I've told the American people, freedom and fear are at war. We face enemies that hate not our policies but our existence, the tolerance of openness and creative culture that defines us. But the outcome of this conflict is certain. There is a current in history, and it runs toward freedom. Our enemies resent it and dismiss it, but the dreams of mankind are defined by liberty, the natural right to create and build and worship and live in dignity. When men and women are released from oppression and isolation, they find fulfillment and hope, and they leave poverty by the millions.

In his famous "Axis of Evil" State of the Union speech on January 29, 2002, Bush continued with the same themes. In that speech, Bush rightfully touted his administration's accomplishments of the previous four months:

We last met in an hour of shock and suffering. In four short months, our nation has comforted the victims, begun to rebuild New York and the Pentagon, rallied a great coalition, captured, arrested, and rid the world of thousands of terrorists, destroyed Afghanistan's terrorist training camps, saved a people from starvation, and freed a country from brutal oppression.

The record was as clear as it was good, and almost all of it was accomplished by the government. Moreover, in that same speech, Bush noted that besides all the new planes, tanks, and airport security measures, he believed that:

Our country also needs citizens working to rebuild our communities. We need mentors to love children, especially children whose parents are in prison. And we need more talented teachers in troubled schools. USA Freedom Corps will expand and improve the good efforts of AmeriCorps and Senior Corps to recruit more than 200,000 new volunteers. And America needs citizens to extend the compassion of our country to every part of the world. So we will renew the promise of the Peace Corps, double its volunteers over the next five years—(applause)—and ask it to join a new effort to encourage development and education and opportunity in the Islamic world.

Except for a possibly hidden agenda to transfer this work to "faith-based" groups, this was a far cry from the typical Conservative campaign speech that attacks the Liberal idea that educating and mentoring our children actually increases national security. Bush's speech then returned to the theme that it is our duty to expand freedom, and that our goals are universal:

> No nation owns these aspirations, and no nation is exempt from them. We have no intention of imposing our culture. But America will always stand firm for the non-negotiable demands of human dignity: the rule of law; limits on the power of the state; respect for women; private property; free speech; equal justice; and religious tolerance.[4]

After all the resistance, and all the attacks against Liberals by Conservatives, human dignity topped the list in a Conservative's speech about what America considers non-negotiable demands. If the words came from Jimmy Carter, Conservatives would have called him a utopian dreamer.

Thus, George W. Bush launched his strategy correctly, by trying to concentrate on unifying his own country and the rest of the world. Conservatives speak in favor of "unilateralism" a lot these days, as if that were a purposeful goal. This is a big mistake. Unilateralism is sometimes necessary: if there is an external threat, we have to protect ourselves as well as we can, even if nobody is willing or able to help us. But unilateralism itself is generally not a proper *goal*, although it certainly appears to be one of Bush's.

Although we should aggressively protect America, our attempts will likely end in failure or a divided country if we do not follow our own Constitutional procedures. Yet, with their incessant invocations of a jingoistic patriotism, and calling into question the loyalty of those who disagree with them, Conservatives unwisely undermine national unity and demonstrate that they use foreign policy to advance their domestic agenda and do not have a due respect for the Constitution.

The Conservative "Strict Constructionists" Don't Believe In The Constitution's War Power Provisions

Liberals also insist upon the strict construction of our liberal national Constitution when it comes to the war-making powers it grants. In carrying out our nation's foreign policy, we should not throw overboard our Constitution, as

---

4.   "State of the Union Address," *BushCountry.org.*, January 29, 2002, at
      http://www.bushcountry.org/bush_speeches/
      president_bush_speech_012902.htm

have both Liberal and Conservative Presidents. It is a source of consternation that Conservatives who so harshly apply the whip to the high horse of "strict construction" are so easily led around by a President waving the flag.

When Reagan came to the White House, our main foreign policy problem was not Iran, China, or even the Soviet Union. Our main problem was that foreign policy was continually tainted by domestic politics. Domestic policy considerations are a legitimate component of foreign policy decisions. After all, the wisdom of a leader is reflected in part by the leader's understanding in advance how a nation's people will react to foreign policy decisions. A foreign intervention can lead to domestic riots or even insurrection if the intervention if things do not turn out well. This is true even for extremely stable political systems such as our own, as the domestic turmoil during the Vietnam war attests. To the extent that citizens holding one view on an issue tend to group together with others who think similarly, often in organizations we call political parties, some overlap between foreign policy issues and party politics should be expected.

However, as the Iran-Contra debate demonstrated, domestic policy agreement and party affiliation can often impede proper decision-making. The Congressional debates over assistance to the Contras were disdainful because the relationship of representatives of both parties' actual views to their eventual votes appeared coincidental, at best. In that matter of life and death, the issue came down to "right-wing for" and "left-wing against." This partisan philosophy of "my party, may it always be right, but my party, right or wrong," has no place in the policies affecting our country's safety.

Whatever else its merits or flaws, the First Gulf War, for the first time since Vietnam, inspired an actual debate in Congress over whether the President's desire to go to war with Iraq was *wise*. Though most Conservatives eventually supported the First Iraq War and most Liberals did not, for once there was a significant overlap.

The power to declare war is the subject of Article I, Section 8 of the Constitution, which provides Congress shall have power:

(11) To declare war, grant letters of marque and reprisal, and make rules concerning captures on land and water.[5]

Oddly, Conservatives are afraid of this provision, as demonstrated by their attacks on the patriotism of those who believe in carrying out the Constitution's mandate that Congress decide the issue, rather than the President, as representative of the executive branch of government. Conservatives do not believe in "discussion" of foreign policy issues, because they believe in playing "follow the leader." This is an unwise way to go about foreign policy, especially when making war. In World War I, the Germans followed their leader into Serbia; millions of patriotic Germans, Frenchmen, Englishmen, Russians, Americans, and others, along with those who were not so patriotic, fought and died in that war. However, instead of that war making the world safe for democracy, Americans found that it had made the world safe for the incubation of the dictatorial mass-murderers who were then followed blindly into an even greater abyss. So, the wise thing for the world would have been for the anti-war folks of all the participating countries to keep their leaders in line and tell them, "Hell, no, we won't go." Mere nationalism has its place in the patriotic quiver, but it can become a very dangerous explosive for our country and the world.

Rather than the obsequious blind faith in a President's foreign policy adventures as advocated by Conservatives such as Coulter, Americans should get down on their knees and thank every dissenter in every war for pointing out the possibly terrible consequences of foreign military action. Conservative members of Congress trot out the "unpatriotic" label, but this is only proof that when Conservatives say they put a lot of stock in the Constitution, they must mean Enron stock, because they seem to believe that Congress should act like the Enron Board of Directors and rubber stamp every proposal made by a chief executive.[6]

---

5.   This provision ends "the Guantanamo debate." Under the general war powers provision, Congress, not the President, makes the law concerning those taken prisoner during war. If there is a difference between a regular enemy soldier, an irregular, and a simple "enemy combatant," George Bush cannot make rules about those differences—only Congress can.

6.   The Conservative charlatans are promoting the idea that we can run the world's biggest empire, with a military out-lay greater than the next 20 countries' *combined*, without collecting taxes from people like Enron's Kenny Boy Lay or Congressman Tom DeLay.

Let's take a real-world look at how the Conservative war-power philosophy subverts the Constitution. Coulter calls Liberals treasonous because:

> Democrats made a big point of opposing every anti-terrorism initiative on the grounds that Bush should be single-mindedly focused on capturing Osama bin Laden. They seem to imagine that President Bush was supposed to be spending his time in Arab bazaars offering bribes to people who might have known where Osama was.[7]

On the micro-scale, Coulter disregards that it was President Bush who told the American people, who then believed him, that it was a high priority to bring back Osama bin Laden "dead or alive." On the macro-scale, every nation on earth has limited resources, even the United States. It was a legitimate question whether the United States could pursue both the war in Afghanistan, including the search for Osama, and a war in Iraq. It is a certainty that Bush's team explored that very issue in depth. It was Congress's duty to investigate, and then either agree or disagree with, the Bush proposition that both goals could be accomplished simultaneously within the limits of acceptable risk. The saying that when it comes to foreign policy, "partisanship ends at the water's edge," does not mean that members of Congress give up their right to advise and consent when they cross over the Potomac into Washington.

Conservatives questioned Liberals' patriotism for wanting the truth about a connection between Al Qaeda and Sadaam Hussein and evidence of Iraq's weapons of mass destruction before going to war. A workable standard for the amount of evidence needed by the President to recommend military action based upon another country's potential use of weapons of mass destruction is akin to what a lawyer must show a judge to obtain a preliminary injunction, which is the reasonable "likelihood" to prevail on the merits when the case is actually tried. This standard sounds a lot higher than it is. The requirement is barely anything more than just a little evidence. This standard means our President can be wrong, but cannot go off half-cocked. But it is higher for showing a "connection" between Al Qaeda and Sadaam Hussein than for weapons of mass destruction, because a "connection," and the "threat" arising from the connection are much more amorphous than the possible existence of weapons. On both counts, *if* Bush actually believed what he said, then he had enough "evidence," and the war was justified. Others who disagreed with Bush

---

7.   Couter, *Treason*, 206

had something important to say, and something for Congress to consider. It was their duty to warn of a possible quagmire and to question whether the threats from both weapons of mass destruction and a possible Al Qaeda connection were erroneous.

Even *without* any weapons of mass destruction or connection to Al Qaeda, there was a significant case to be made for war against Iraq for the reason belatedly given by Bush—the mass murders. Dictatorships are not governments—they are criminal enterprises. In North Korea, one of the "axis of evil" countries, for instance, the esteemed magazine *The Economist* noted, "There is the awful fact that 50 years of Kim family rule have produced seven-year-olds who are on average eight inches shorter and 22 pounds lighter than their potential South Korean playmates whom they are still forbidden to meet."[8] Such a regime has no right to exist. Therefore, it may be removed in "police action" wars just like an ordinary criminal. This is the strength of the "go to the UN first" argument. It is not that the United States should cede its sovereignty to the UN for a defensive war, even if the defense is preemption. Rather, where there is no threat externally from the dictatorship but the enemy government is a threat only to its own people, it is far better to persuade the world that the UN—as the symbolic world cop—should sanction the war. Even without UN sanction (and Bush made a good case that the war was, in fact, UN-sanctioned), the United States might have good cause to fight a war to rid the world of a dictator. That is what we legitimately did in Kosovo, with the assistance of our NATO allies.

But, justification for the war hinges upon the "if"—"*if* Bush actually believed what he said." That Bush *could* have made a case for war based upon the cruelty of Sadaam Hussein's dictatorship does not mean he did. Bush insisted we go to war because of the threat Hussein's weapons of mass destruction posed and because of Hussein's supposed connections with Al Qaeda and 9/11. *If* Bush believe these threats loomed, he was entitled to a good-faith mistake in urging war, even though his reasons may be proven to be based upon the erroneous intelligence before him at the time.

However, Bush was *not* entitled to lie as to the reasons to go to war against Iraq, even if there were other valid reasons. If Bush trumped up the weapons of mass destruction threat or the Al Qaeda connection, he should be impeached. Conservatives labeled Clinton's Kosovo bombing "wag the dog"

---

8.   "Nuclear Futures," *The Economist*, January 24-30, 2004, 74.

and called for his impeachment. If that bombing had been an example of wag the dog, then the Conservatives' demand would have been correct, but in that case there was no evidence to support the Conservatives' theory. The question is whether there is anything more than a little evidence to support Bush's stated reasons for the war. The resignation of David Kay, Bush's chief weapons inspector, who stated that his mission was about 85% completed—with still no WMDs found—raises a serious doubt about Bush's motivations. Perhaps revenge for Hussein's attack on Bush's father was indeed the cause. If so, none of the other reasons matters, and Bush should be thrown from office, even though *at the time* the attack on his father alone justified a war against Iraq. Old offenses do not justify a war; only new provocations do.

But Liberals were too quick to jump on the concept of preemptive war, because preemption is not the issue. The real issue is identifying which threats can be met with preemption, because sometimes a threat is the same thing as an attack. No country has to wait until the launch of a nuclear ICBM against it to defend itself. So at what point is preemption reasonable? Is the danger high enough when another country hires the first nuclear scientist with the actual intent to invent a nuclear weapon to launch at us? The answer necessarily depends on whether the nuclear scientist is Albert Einstein or Mr. Bean. Excluding the pacifist, everyone will agree that self-defense allows preemptive and unilateral military action when another nation is preparing an attack against the United States, because at some point the preparation and the actual attack from abroad cease to be two distinct things.

Attacking critics in Congress for speaking their minds on these subjects is divisive and anti-Constitutional, because it is their solemn duty to do so. It is also entirely anti-ethical and anti-religious, because before governments send or authorize the sending of other human beings into harm's way, they'd better have weighed the consequences, the advice they have received, and their own consciences. And, certainly, the Conservative goal of acting unilaterally abroad, while dividing the home base into loyalists and traitors, is national suicide in the making.

CONCLUSION

At home and abroad, Liberalism is clearly the right path for America. Domestically, it uses Lincoln and Roosevelt's instrument of the people—our federal government—to promote both individual *and* general welfare. In the past, this has enabled us to break the bonds of slavery, to overcome Jim Crow, to ensure the safety of our food and banks and the fairness of our commerce, and to protect our old, sick, and poor. In the future, it will allow us to properly regulate guns and to provide better and more equitable health care and education. Overseas, only Liberalism can convince all the troops that they are fighting for something in which every one of them has a stake. This is why Liberals have led all of this country's victorious major war campaigns. Liberalism is truly the only philosophy that fights for all of America. So whether you are motivated by self-interest or the common interest—

You either are a Liberal, or you should be.

APPENDIX A

FEDERALIST SOCIETY MEMBERS

As related by:
People For the American Way, 2000 M Street, NW, Suite 400
http://www.pfaw.org/pfaw/general/default.aspx?oid=780

James Bopp, General Counsel to the National Right to Life Committee, the James Madison Center for Free Speech, and former counsel to the Christian Coalition

Judge Robert Bork, failed Supreme Court nominee

Michael Carvin, former Assistant Deputy Attorney General in the Justice Department under President Reagan.

Gail Heriot, who co-chaired the campaign supporting California's Proposition 209

Linda Chavez, President of the Center for Equal Opportunity, an organization dedicated to fighting affirmative action programs

Roger Clegg, Vice President and General Counsel for the Center for Equal Opportunity

Charles Cooper, former Assistant Attorney General, Office of Legal Counsel under Ronald Reagan

Maura Corrigan, Michigan Supreme Court Chief Justice

Frank Easterbrook, Judge on the United States Court of Appeals for the Seventh Circuit

John Engler, Governor, State of Michigan

Richard Epstein, law professor at the University of Chicago Law School, author of *Forbidden Grounds: The Case Against Employment Discrimination Laws and Takings: Private Property and the Power of Eminent Domain*

Thomas F. Gede, former Assistant Attorney General, State of California

Lino Graglia, University of Texas law professor and ardent opponent of affirmative action

C. Boyden Gray, former White House Counsel to George H.W. Bush during his terms as president and vice president. He is now the Chairman of Citizens for a Sound Economy

Senator Orrin Hatch, ranking Republican on the Senate Judiciary Committee

Don Hodel, former President of the Christian Coalition

Lynn Hogue, Chairman of the Legal Advisory Board of the Southeastern Legal Foundation who led the charge to get former President Clinton disbarred

Alan G. Lance, Attorney General, State of Idaho

Stephen Markman, Michigan Supreme Court Justice

Nancie Marzulla, President of Defenders of Property Rights

Roger Marzulla, General Counsel and Chairman of the Board of Directors of Defenders of Property Rights

Charles Murray, author of *The Bell Curve*, a 1994 book that asserted that some races are inherently less intelligent than others

Robert Natelson, senior fellow at the Independence Institute

David Owsiany, Chief of Policy and Research for the Ohio Department of Insurance

Richard Posner, Judge on the U.S. Court of Appeals for the Seventh Circuit and a senior lecturer at the University of Chicago Law School

William Pryor, Attorney General, State of Alabama

Grover Rees III, special assistant for judicial selection under former Attorney General Edwin Meese.

Antonin Scalia, Supreme Court Justice

David Sentelle, protoge of Sen. Jesse Helms who was appointed to the Special Division, the three judge panel responsible for overseeing the investigations of the Independent Counsel by Chief Justice William Rehnquist.

Bradley Smith, Member of the Federal Election Commission, Author of Unfree Speech: The Folly of Campaign Finance Reform

Kenneth Starr, former Independent Counsel

Don Stenberg, Attorney General, State of Nebraska

Clifford Taylor, Michigan Supreme Court Justice

Richard Thornburgh, former U.S. Attorney General and former Governor of the State of Pennsylvania

David Wagner, former Director of Legal Policy for the Family Research Council

Elizabeth Weaver, Michigan Supreme Court Justice

Robert Young, Michigan Supreme Court Justice[1]

---

1. People For the American Way 2000 M Street, NW, Suite 400 http://www.pfaw.org/pfaw/general/default.aspx?oid=780

Appendix B

McCARTHYISM CHRONOLOGY

As related by:
http://history.acusd.edu/gen/20th/1950s/mccarthy.html

1950 Jan. 7 meeting at the Colony restaurant, agreed to lead Republican investigation of communism in Truman administration.

Feb. 9 Wheeling speech to Republican Women's Club at the McClure Hotel, said he had a list of 205 names of communists in the State Dept.

Feb. 10 Salt Lake City speech said he had 57 names.

Feb. 20 Senate speech for six hours, said he had 81 names, including "one of our foreign ministers."

Feb. 22 at the suggestion of Senate Majority Leader Scott Lucas, the Tyding Committee was created of 5 members, a subcommittee of the Foreign Relations Committee, to investigate McCarthy's accusations.

Mar. 8 Tydings Committee began hearings, McCarthy entered at 10 am with big brown briefcase, said he was prepared to make big revelations

Mar. 30 McCarthy accused Owen Lattimore, Far Eastern expert at Johns Hopkins, but the Tydings Committee cleared Lattimore by Apr. 6.

June 1 speech in Senate by Maggie Smith denounced McCarthy.

June 21 publication of Red Channels alleging Communist affiliations of 151 entertainers started the Blacklist.

July 20 report by Tydings Committee denounced McCarthy.

Oct. midterm elections gave McCarthy the opportunity to attack the Democrats, especially members of the Tydings Committeee; used false picture associating Millard Tydings with Earl Browder, and Tydings was defeated in Maryland by Republican John Marshall Butler; Senate Majority Leader Scott Lucas was defeated in Illinois by Republican Everett Dirksen; Republicans won 5 seats in the Senate and 28 seats in the House, and McCarthy received $200,000 that was deposited in his personal checking account.

1951 June 14 report by McCarthy of 60,000 words attacked George Marshall as an "instrument of a Soviet conspiracy."

Aug. 6 resolution introduced by Sen. William Benton to expel McCarthy, but nothing done after 16-month investigation by the Rules Committee; Benton lost the Connecticut election in 1952!

Oct. 28 speech by McCarthy attacked Adlai Stevenson.

Dec. incident at a Washington DC party where McCarthy slapped and kicked columnist Drew Pearson.

1953 As January session of Congress opened, McCarthy was appointed chairman of the Senate Committee on Government Operations, where according to Robert Taft "he can't do any harm."

Mar. 12 speech opposed nomination of Charles Bohlen to be ambassador to Russia, followed by series of speeches attacking the State Department overseas libraries and the Voice of America.

July notification of induction into the Army sent to G. David Schine, heir to hotel fortune, friend of McCarthy Committee counsel Roy Cohn and unpaid consultant for the Committee.

Oct investigation by McCarthy of the Army Signal Corps at Fort Monmouth, soon expanded to investigate other Army operations, including the Army's honorable discharge of Capt. Irving Peress, Army dentist who refused to answer his loyalty questionnaire in 1952.

Nov. 24 attack on Eisenhower administration, began to carry .45 automatic pistol.

1954 Jan. Gallup poll gave McCarthy a public approval rating of 50%, was given a seat on the Senate Rules Committee, at height of his influence.

Feb. 24 agreement by Secretary of the Army Robert Stevens to allow Gen. Ralph Zwicker, the commanding officer of Peress, to testify before McCarthy's Committee

Mar. 8 began Edward R. Murrow's "See It Now" documentary on McCarthy.

Mar. 11 report by Army showed 44 efforts by McCarthy staff members Roy Cohn and Francis Carr to get preferential treatment for Private Schine.

Apr. 22 began the Army-McCarthy hearings, televised live for 36 days to an audience of 20 million; kinescopes of these hearing were used by Emile de Antonio to produce the 1964 documentary "Point of Order."

Dec. 2 condemnation by Senate.

1957 May death of McCarthy from cirrhosis of the liver[1]

---

1.   http://history.acusd.edu/gen/20th/1950s/mccarthy.html

APPENDIX C

WATERGATE CHRONOLOGY

As related by:
http://www.people.memphis.edu/~sherman/chronoWatergate.htm

1970

July 14: Nixon approves Huston Plan (formulated by Tom Charles Huston, a White House aide with an ambition to gain control of all domestic intelligence), which proposed using burglary, illegal electronic surveillance, the opening of mail, among other methods, to control domestic opponents of the administration.

July 28: Nixon withdraws approval of the Huston Plan because of opposition by FBI director J. Edgar Hoover who feared exposure by the press or congressional investigation.

1971

June 13: The New York Times begins printing the Pentagon Papers, a Robert McNamara-commissioned study of America's role in Vietnam. Daniel Ellsberg, a Pentagon bureaucrat who worked on the project and changed from a supporter to an opponent of the war as a result, save the material to the Times, who planned to publish a series of articles based upon the report.

June 17: After the first three articles appeared, the Justice Department issued a restraining order to halt further publication, arguing that this would cause "immediate and irreparable harm" to national defense.

143

June 30: The Supreme Court denied the Nixon administration's attempt at prior restraint, ruling that the First Amendment guarantee of a free press overrode the government's claim.

Sept 3-4: Plumbers, a private intelligence group in the White House intended to plug leaks to the media, (a group which included former CIA operatives with histories of involvement in the Bay of Pigs and the coup in Guatemala in 1954) burglarize the office of Daniel Ellsberg's psychiatrist, seeking material to discredit Ellsberg and the antiwar movement.

1972

January 17: Harris Poll reveals that if election were held today the electorate was evenly split: 42% for Nixon, 42% for Muskie.

January 27: Liddy presents his $1 million plan, code named Gemstone, that included break-ins, wiretapping, sabotage, kidnapping, mugging squads and the use of prostitutes for political blackmail. After a bit of adjustments, including halving the budget, the group (including Attorney General John Mitchell, John Dean, and Jeb Magruder) agreed on three priorities: Lawrence O'Brien's office as chairman of the Democratic National Committee (located in the Watergate office complex), O'Brien's hotel suite at the convention, and the headquaters of whoever became the Democratic nominee.

March 1: John Mitchell becomes chairman of the Committee to Re-elect the President (CREEP). Richard Kleindienst is appointed to replace him.

April 27: The victim of a host of "dirty tricks," Edmund S. Muskie withdraws from the campaign to win the Democratic nomination for president.

May: The Plumbers attempt three times to break into the Democratic National Committee headquarters at the Watergate. The third time they are successful, photocopying documents and installing telephone taps. Plumbers fail in two attempt to break into the headquarters of George McGovern. They break into the embassy of Chile in hopes that the FBI will consider all break-ins as the work of the CIA.

June 17: At the Watergate Office Building in Washington, D.C., five men are arrested during a pathetically bungled break-in at the offices of the Democratic National Committee (DNC). The men are all carrying cash and documents that show them to be employed by the Committee to Re-elect the President, and the purpose of the burglary is to plant listening devices in the phones of the Democratic leaders and obtain political documents regarding the Democrats' campaign strategy. The men arrested include a former FBI agent and four anti-Castro Cubans who have been told that they are looking for material linking Castro to the Democratic Party. Two former White House aides working for CREEP, G. Gordon Liddy and E. Howard Hunt, are also arrested. Hunt, it will be learned, was one of the CIA agents responsible for planning the Bay of Pigs invasion and some of the Cubans arrested also took part in the invasion. The seven men are indicted on September 15. Even though their relationship to the election committee is established, none of the seven men connects the committee or the White House to the break-in.

June 21: John Mitchell reports publicly that neither the White House nor CREEP is connected to the break-in.

June 23: Nixon and his chief of staff, John Erlichmann, formulate a plan to have the CIA call off the FBI investigation of the break-in. Nixon's taping system records the conversation that will prove to be the "smoking gun" of the Watergate investigation.

August 29: Nixon states "categorically" that the White House is not involved with the break-in.

September 15: A federal grand jury indicts the five Watergate burglars and E. Howard Hunt and G. Gordon Liddy.

October 10: The Washington Post reports that CREEP and the White House control a secret fund that financed a campaign of political sabotage, including the Watergate break-in.

November 7: After an October Gallup poll shows that less than half of the American people have even heard of the break-in, President Nixon defeats his Democratic challenger, Senator George McGovern, in a landslide, capturing 60.8 percent of the popular vote and 520 or the 537 electoral votes. McGovern carries only Massachusetts and Washington, D.C.

December 8: The wife of E. Howard Hunt dies in a plane crash in Chicago. She is carrying $10,000 in $100 bills. The money is "hush money" she was ferrying to someone in Chicago.

1973

January 10-30: In the trial of the Watergate burglars under Judge John J. Sirica, five of the indicted plead guilty and the jury convicts Liddy and James McCord, director of CREEP security.

January: Gallup Poll reveals 68 percent approve of Nixon's "handling his job as President."

February 7: Amid swirling rumors of widespread wrongdoing, corrupt financing, and political dirty tricks committed by the Nixon reelection committee, the Senate votes 77-0 to establish a Select Committee on Presidential Campaign Activities, chaired by North Carolina Senator Sam Ervin.

March 23: Former CIA agent James W. McCord, one of the seven men convicted in the attempted burglary, admits in a letter to Judge John Sirica that he and other defendants have been under pressure to remain silent about the case. McCord reveals that others were involved in the break-in, and he eventually names John Mitchell, the former Attorney General who had become chairman of the Committee to Re-elect the President, as the "overall boss."

April 20: L. Patrick Gray, acting director of the FBI, resigns after admitting he destroyed evidence connected to Watergate, on the advice of Nixon aides in the White House.

April 30: Nixon's chief of staff, H.R. Haldeman, domestic affairs assistant John Erlichman, and Attorney General Richard Kleindienst are forced to resign; presidential counsel John Dean III is fired. In a televised speech announcing the shake-up, President Nixon denies any knowledge of the cover-up of White House involvement in the Watergate break-in.

May 11: Charges against Daniel Ellsberg and Anthony J. Russo for their theft and release of the Pentagon Papers are dropped. The judge makes this decision following the revelation that Watergate conspirators E. Howard Hunt and G. Gordon Liddy had burglarized the office of Ellsberg's psychiatrist in an attempt to steal Ellsberg's medical records.

May 17: The Senate Watergate Committee, chaired by Sam Ervin, begins televised hearings.

May 18: Attorney General Elliot Richardson, who replaced Kleindienst, names Harvard Law School professor Archibald Cox as special prosecutor.

June 25: Testifying before Ervin's Senate committee, John Dean accuses President Nixon of involvement in the Watergate cover-up and says the President authorized payment of "hush money" to the seven men arrested in the break-in.

July 16: In startling testimony, White House aide Alexander Butterfield tells the Ervin committee that President Nixon secretly recorded all Oval Office conversations. This revelation provides the committee with the means to substantiate testimony implicating the President in the cover-up of the Watergate burglary. It also sets off a constitutional crisis over the President's right to keep the tapes secret under the umbrella of "executive privilege."

July 16-25: The Senate Committee and Cox supoena tapes of some White House conversations. Nixon refuses, citing executive privilege.

August 29: Judge Sirica rules that Nixon must turn over the tapes. Nixon appeals.

September: Harris Poll: If you had it to do over again, for whom would you vote for President in 1972? McGovern, 38%; Nixon, 36%; neither 11%.

October 10: In an unrelated development that further damages White House credibility, Vice President Spiro Agnew, the chief voice for "law and order" in the Nixon White House, resigns after pleading nolo contendere (no contest) to tax-evasion charges dating from his days as governor of Maryland. Two days later, Nixon nominates House Minority Leader Gerald Ford to succeed Agnew under the provisions of the Twenty-fifth Amendment, allowing the President to fill a vacancy in the vice presidency.

October 20: "The Saturday Night Massacre." President Nixon orders Attorney General Elliot Richardson to fire Watergate Special Prosecutor Archibald Cox, who has refused to accept the President's compromise offer to release a "synopsis"of the tapes. Richardson and his assistant, William D. Ruckelshaus, refuse to follow this order and both resign.

Solicitor General Robert Bork, third in the Justice Department chain of command, fires Cox. (The Democrat's revenge will come when Ronald Reagan nominates Bork to the Supreme Court in 1988. Bork's nomination will open an acrimonious debate over his legal views, and he will be rejected by the Senate.) The resignations and the firing of Cox raise a storm of protest in Congress, and the House actively begins to consider impeachment of the President.

October 23: The House Judiciary Committee, chaired by Representative Peter Rodino, announces an investigation into impeachment charges against the President. Leon Jaworski is appointed special prosecutor in the Watergate investigation to replace Archibald Cox.

October 30: After Nixon reluctantly agrees to turn over the Oval Office tapes, investigators learn that two tapes are missing.

November 9: Six of the Watergate defendants are sentenced for their roles in the break-in. G. Gordon Liddy is sentenced to twenty years, in part because of his refusal to cooperate with investigators. E. Howard Hunt receives a sentence of two and a half to eight years and a $10,000 fine. The others are given lesser sentences.

November 13: Representatives of two oil companies plead guilty to making illegal contributions to the Nixon campaign. The next day, Commerce Secretary Maurice Stans, who was the Nixon campaign treasurer, admits that such contributions were expected from major corporations. Two days later, three more companies—Goodyear, Braniff Airlines, and American Airlines—report similar donations.

November 21: Investigators learn that one of the tapes contains a mysterious eighteen-and-a-half-minute gap. The White House claims that Rosemary Woods, Nixon's secretary, accidentally erased part of the tape while transcribing it, a feat that, owing to the way the recording apparatus was set up, would have required the skills of a contortionist. (In January 1974, analysis of the tape will show that the erasure was deliberate—the result of five separate manual erasures.)

November 30: Egil Krogh, Jr., who headed the White House "plumbers" unit, pleads guilty to charges stemming from the break-in at the offices of Daniel Ellsberg's psychiatrist.

December 6: Gerald Ford is sworn in as Vice President. Besides having been a member of the Warren Commission investigating the death of President Kennedy, Ford is best known for what Lyndon Johnson once said about him: "Shucks, I don't think he can chew gum and walk at the same time…He's a nice fellow, but he spent too much time playing football without a helmet."

1974

January 4: Claiming "executive privilege," President Nixon refuses to surrender five hundred tapes and documents subpoenaed by the Senate Watergate Committee.

February 6: The House of Representatives votes 410-4 to begin formal impeachment inquiry.

March 1: Seven former White House staff members, including Haldeman, Ehrlichman, and former Attorney General John Mitchell, are indicted for conspiring to obstruct the investigation of the Watergate break-in. The grand jury names Nixon an unindicted coconspirator but withholds this information from the public.

April 3: Following months of investigation by a separate congressional committee, President Nixon agrees to pay more than $400,000 in back taxes. Using suspect deductions, the President had paid taxes equivalent to those levied on a salary of $15,000, despite the President's $200,000 salary and other income.

April 11: House Judiciary Committee votes 33-3 to subpoena 42 tapes. Nixon refuses to release them.

April 30: In another nationally televised address, President Nixon offers a 1,308 page edited transcript of the tapes subpoenaed by the House Judiciary Committee and Special Prosecutor Jaworski. Both Jaworski and the committee reject the transcripts.

May 9: Republican leader of the House, John J. Rhodes, announces that Nixon should consider resignation.

May 16: Richard Kleindienst, John Mitchell's successor as Attorney General, pleads guilty to a misdemeanor charge of failing to testify accurately before a Senate committee. Kleindienst is the first Attorney General ever convicted of a crime.

May 24: Special Prosecutor Jaworski appeals to the Supreme Court for a ruling on his subpoena for the president to release to him 64 recorded conversations.

July 24: The Supreme Court rules unanimously that Nixon must turn over the tapes requested by the special prosecutor. Eight hours later, the White House announces it will comply with the order.

July 27: The House Judiciary Committee first of the articles of impeachment against Nixon, charging him with obstructing justice. Six Republicans vote for the articles.

July 29: The Judiciary Committee passes its second impeachment article 22-10 for abuse of power.

July 30: Judiciary Committee passes third article of impeachment 21-17 for defying House subpoenas.

July 31: For his crimes of perjury and conspiracy, John Erlichmann is sentenced to prison.

August 2: For his role in the cover-up, John Dean receives a prison sentence.

August 5: In another televised address, Nixon releases transcripts of a conversation with chief of staff Haldeman. The transcript shows that, six days after the break-in, Nixon ordered a halt to the FBI investigation of the affair. Nixon concedes that he failed to include this information in earlier statements, what he calls "a serious omission." This is the "smoking gun" that everybody has been looking for. Following the speech, Nixon's remaining congressional support disappears; key Republican congressmen tell him he will probably be impeached and convicted.

August 6: Every Republican member of the House Judiciary Committee, all of whom are lawyers, state that they will vote to impeach the president. Only two members in the House of Representatives announce that they will vote against impeachment.

August 8: President Nixon announces his resignation, effective noon the following day. A Gallup Poll indicates 65% of Americans support impeachment.

August 9: President Nixon formally resigns and leaves for California. Vice President Gerald Ford is sworn in as President.

August 21: President Ford nominates Nelson Rockefeller, the governor of New York and three-time candidate for the Republican presidential nomination, as his choice for Vice President.

September 8: President Ford grants Richard Nixon a "full, free and absolute pardon...for all offenses against the United States which he...has committed or may have committed or taken part in while President."

1975

January 1: Four of the former White House staffers charged with obstruction are found guilty. They are H.R. Haldeman, John Ehrlichman, John Mitchell, and Robert Mardian. A fifth, Kenneth Parkinson, is acquitted. The Watergate charges against Charles Colson are dropped after he pleads guilty to crimes connected with the Ellsberg-psychiatrist break-in. A seventh defendant, Gordon Strachan, is tried separately.

1976

In the presidential election this year, Jimmy Carter narrowly defeats President Ford. Besides the economic problems facing the country, Carter's victory is widely attributed to the post-Watergate atmosphere of cynicism and a very specific rejection of Ford for his pardon of Nixon. The final accounting of the Watergate affair produces an impressive list of "high crimes and misdemeanors," as the Constitution labels impeachable offenses. But others were offenses against the law, against individual citizens, and against the Constitution of the United States itself.[1]

---

1. http://www.people.memphis.edu/~sherman/chronoWatergate.htm

APPENDIX D

ARMED SERVICES ROSTERS

As related by:
http://www.bartcop.com/warvets.htm

Republicans:

Elliott Abrams—Sought deferment for bad back.
Richard Armey—Sought college deferment, too smart to die.
Bill Bennett—Sought graduate school deferment, too smart to die.
George W. Bush—Daddy got him in the National Guard, went AWOL
Dick Cheney—Sought graduate school deferment, too smart to die.
Tom DeLay—Sought college deferment, too smart to die.
Newt Gingrich—Sought graduate school deferment, too smart to die.
Phil Gramm—Sought marriage deferment, too loved to die.
Ronald Reagan—served in a noncombat role during WWII in the states. He later seems to have confused his role as an actor playing a tail gunner with the real thing.
Bob Dornan—avoided Korean War combat duty by enrolling in college acting classes
Phil Gramm—avoided the draft, did not serve, four (?) student deferments
Senator John McCain—McCain's naval honors include the Silver Star, Bronze Star, Legion of Merit, Purple Heart and Distinguished Flying Cross.
Former Senator Bob Dole—an honorable man Served in WWII and severely wounded.
Chuck Hagel—two Purple Hearts and a Bronze Star, Vietnam.

Duke Cunningham—nominated for the Medal of Honor, received the Navy Cross, two Silver Stars, fifteen Air Medals, the Purple Heart, and several other decorations

Rush Limbaugh—Sought deferment for ingrown hair follicle on his ass.

Trent Lott—Sought deferment, didn't want to muss his hair.

P.J. O'Rourke—Sought deferment, too stoned.

Kenneth Starr Sought deferment for psoriasis.

John Wayne—Sought deferment to further acting career.

Vin Weber—Sought deferment for asthma.

George Will—Sought deferment, too much of a wussy.

Don Nickles, Senate Minority Whip—Did not serve

Senator Richard Shelby, did not serve

Saxby Chambliss, Georgia—did not serve, had a "bad knee" (yet somehow feels he has a right to attack Max Cleland's patriotism)

Representative JC Watts—did not serve Jack Kemp, did not serve (was fit enough for pro football, but "failed" the physical?)

Dan Quayle, avoided Vietnam service, got a slot in the journalism unit of the Indiana National Guard when the unit was at 150% capacity (at least he showed up for his duty, unlike GW)

Karl Rove—avoided the draft, did not serve, too busy being a Republican.

Eliot Abrams, did not serve

Vin Weber, did not serve

Richard Perle, did not serve (is the current bloodshed in the Middle East a direct result of his treasonous meddling in Clinton Administration foreign policy?)

Rudy Giuliani, did not serve

Att'y Gen. John Ashcroft—sought deferment to teach business ed at SW Missouri State

John Engler, did not serve

Tom Ridge, Bronze Star for Valor in Vietnam

Sam R. Johnson, combat missions in both Korea and Vietnam, POW in Hanoi from April 1966 to February 1973 (don't ever run for president Sam, they'll spread rumors that you're crazy)

Speaker of the House Dennis Hastert—avoided the draft, did not serve.

Punditocracy and Preacher-types:

George Will, did not serve

Bill O'Reilly, did not serve

Paul Gigot, did not serve.

Bill Bennett, Did not serve

Pat Buchanan, did not serve

Pat Robertson—did not serve, apparently used Daddy's connections to get off the ship
in Tokyo while his buddies went on to Korea.

Bill Kristol, did not serve

Independents

Gov. Jesse Ventura, U.S. Navy SEAL training, did UDT work

Senator Jim Jeffords, U.S. Navy 1956-1959

Prominent Democrats

Gray Davis, California Governor, served in Vietnam.

Chuck Robb, US Senator from Virginia, served in Vietnam

George McGovern, famous liberal, awarded Silver Star & DFC, dozens of missions during WWII.

Pete Stark, D-CA, served in the Air Force

House Minority Leader Richard Gephardt—Served his country in uniform, 1965-71

House Minority Whip David Bonior—Served his country in uniform, 1968-72

Senate Majority Leader Tom Daschle—Served his country in uniform, 1969-72

Former VP Al Gore—Served his country in uniform, 1969-71; recipient of Vietnam Service Medal

Bob Kerrey...Democrat...Congressional Medal of Honor, Vietnam

Daniel Inouye...Democrat...Congressional Medal of Honor, World War Two

John Kerry...Democrat...Silver Star & Bronze Star, Vietnam

Charles Rangel...Democrat...Bronze Star, Korea

Max Cleland...Democrat...Silver Star & Bronze Star, Vietnam

Howell Heflin...Democrat...Silver Star

Senator Ted Kennedy (D-MA)—U.S. Army, 1951-1953.

Senator Tom Harkin (D-IA)—U.S. Navy, 1962-67; Naval Reserve, 1968-74.

Rep. Leonard Boswell (D-IA)—two tours in Vietnam, two Distinguished Flying Crosses as a helicopter pilot,
two Bronze Stars, and the Soldier's Medal.
Ambassador "Pete" Peterson, Air Force Captain, POW, Democratic congressman, Ambassador to Viet Nam,
and recipient of the Purple Heart, the Silver Star and the Legion of Merit
Rep. Mike Thompson, D-CA: served in combat with the U.S. Army as a staff sergeant/platoon leader
with the 173rd Airborne Brigade; was wounded and received a Purple Heart[1]

---

1.   http://www.bartcop.com/warvets.htm

ABOUT THE AUTHOR

Keevan D. Morgan has been practicing law in Chicago since 1977 and is a founding partner of his current law firm, Morgan & Bley, Ltd. Mr. Morgan holds a bachelor's degree from the University of Wisconsin in Madison, where he graduated with distinction in his major, history, and a law degree from the Washington College of Law of American University in Washington, D.C. His representation of police officers against their own police department and the City of Highland Park, Illinois, who claimed to be retaliated against for speaking out against racial profiling and other alleged infractions was the topic of an NBC TV Dateline program in 2000 and a series of investigative reports by local television stations and other media.

Mr. Morgan has appeared before judges both in and outside his home state at courts that include:

* U.S. Court of Appeals for the 7th Circuit

* U.S. District Courts in Illinois, Wisconsin, and California

* U.S. Bankruptcy Courts in Illinois, Indiana, and Alabama

Well-known at Chicago's federal bankruptcy courts for representing both debtors and creditors, Mr. Morgan enjoys a reputation as an unparalleled strategist and tough litigator, apparently leading at least one person to name a German Shepherd after him. During the past two decades, he has provided legal representation for many banks in and around Chicago.

Mr. Morgan has served on corporate boards since he was 25 yeaers old, including for two national banks, where he held such posts as Chairman of the Community Reinvestment Act Committee which oversaw the establishment and continuation of fair lending practices throughout the bank's designated lending area, and was a member of the Loan Committee and Ethics Committee. Mr. Morgan has also served on the boards of an insurance company, a finance company, and a number of entities trading on the Chicago Board Options Exchange. Mr. Morgan's status as a business "insider" gives him a unique perspective in advocating progressive business and governmental policies, while demonstrating that Conservatives' fawning over business for its own sake is misplaced and ultimately self-defeating, because only a progressive business environment puts everyone "on the team" and that leads to higher profits.

Mr. Morgan is married and has three daughters. He is an avid reader and Civil War buff, and during summers he can be found on the pitching mound of a suburban Chicago modified fast-pitch league where he was 7-0 in 2003, and batted .429.

0-595-31354-X

JUN -. 2005

Printed in the United States
22287LVS00005B/166

9 780595 313549